COMMUNITY LIFE
INNER DEVELOPMENT
SEXUALITY
and the
SPIRITUAL TEACHER

COMMUNITY LIFE INNER DEVELOPMENT SEXUALITY and the SPIRITUAL TEACHER

Ethical and Spiritual Dimensions
of the Crisis in
the Anthroposophical Society,
Dornach, 1915

Lectures and Documents

Rudolf Steiner

Translated by Catherine E. Creeger
Introduction by Christopher Schaefer

ANTHROPOSOPHIC PRESS

THIS BOOK IS A TRANSLATION OF
*PROBLEME DES ZUSAMMENLEBENS IN DER
ANTHROPOSOPHISCHEN GESELLSCHAFT: ZUR DORNACHER KRISE
VOM JAHRE 1915* (VOLUME 253 IN THE COLLECTED WORKS),
PUBLISHED BY RUDOLF STEINER VERLAG,
DORNACH, SWITZERLAND, 1989.

Published in the United States of America
by Anthroposophic Press, Inc.,
R.D. 4, Box 94 A1, Hudson, New York 12534.

© 1991 by Anthroposophic Press, Inc.

Library of Congress Cataloging-in-Publication Data

Steiner, Rudolf, 1861–1925.
    [Probleme des Zusammenlebens in der Anthroposophischen Gesellschaft.
English]
    Community life, inner development, sexuality, and the spiritual teacher :
ethical and spiritual dimensions of the crisis in the Anthroposophical Society,
Dornach, 1915 : lectures and documents /Rudolf Steiner : translated by
Catherine E. Creeger ; introduction by Christopher Schaefer.
    Translation of: Probleme des Zusammenlebens in der Anthroposophischen
Gesellschaft.
    ISBN 0-88010-355-8 — ISBN 0-88010-354-X (pbk.)
    1. Anthroposophy. 2. Psychoanalysis and religion. I. Title.
BP595.S894P75513   1991
299′.935—dc20   91-10663
                                                                                      CIP

PRINTED IN THE UNITED STATES OF AMERICA

Contents

About This Edition

This volume is part of the series of "Writings and Lectures on the History of the Anthroposophical Movement and the Anthroposophical Society," in Rudolf Steiner's collected works (*Gesamtausgabe*). In it, Rudolf Steiner expresses his views on a personal attack on himself that took place in the summer of 1915. Serious accusations had been leveled against him from within the circle of members who had come together around the *Goetheanum* that was then being built and known as the *Johannesbau*. He felt that a thorough clarification was in order and spared no one in analyzing and assessing the case. To gain a clear picture of the situation, it is suggested that readers refer to Part Two for details as they read Part One.

In general, Rudolf Steiner ignored the "mystical eccentricities" of psychologically unstable personalities that are inevitably attracted to spiritual communities. He considered them harmless as long as the community saw them for what they were. However, he had already had to experience on several occasions that members with neurotic tendencies were seen as "apostles," as "beings of a higher sort" by other members of the Society, and the 1915 case was so serious that he felt compelled to ask, "[Are we] allowed to tolerate the fact that our Society and our entire movement are constantly being endangered by all kinds of pathological cases?" (August 22, 1915, see p. 145).

The addresses and comments collected in this volume were intended to lay the groundwork for assessing the case. Rudolf Steiner felt the need to not only expose the subjective roots of the incident, but also to place it in an objective context from a spiritual scientific point of view. Therefore, these lectures have a certain fundamental significance in addition to their import for the history of the Anthroposophical Society. The crisis that came to a head in the summer of 1915 was already looming at Christmas of 1914 and lasted through the fall of 1915. Thus, many if not all of the lectures given in Dornach in 1915 relate to it in some way. In particular, see the volumes:

Wege der geistigen Erkenntnis und der Erneuerung künstlerischer Weltanschauung ("Paths to Spiritual Knowledge and Renewal of Art Philosophy"), GA 161, (Dornach, Switzerland: Rudolf Steiner Verlag, 1980).

Kunst- und Lebensfragen im Lichte der Geisteswissenschaft ("Questions of Art and Life in Light of Spiritual Science"), GA 162, (Dornach, Switzerland: Rudolf Steiner Verlag, 1985).

Chance, Providence and Necessity, GA 163, (Hudson, NY: Anthroposophic Press, 1988).

Der Wert des Denkens für eine den Menschen befriedigende Weltanschauung. Das Verhältnis der Geisteswissenschaft zur Naturwissenschaft ("Thinking's Value for a Humanly Satisfying World View: The Relationship of Spiritual Science to Natural Science"), GA 164, (Dornach, Switzerland: Rudolf Steiner Verlag, 1984).

Die okkulte Bewegung im neunzehnten Jahrhundert und ihre Beziehung zur Weltkultur ("The Occult Movement in the Nineteenth Century and Its Relationship to World Culture"), GA 254 (Dornach, Switzerland: Rudolf Steiner Verlag, 1986).

Introduction

These lectures and documents from the summer and fall of 1915 were a response to a crisis in the Anthroposophical Society, a crisis Rudolf Steiner wanted the membership to be aware of.

In part, the crisis was caused by Alice Sprengel, a long-time student of Rudolf Steiner, and her reaction apparently provoked by the marriage of her spiritual teacher to Marie von Sivers. Her expectations, the exact nature of which is not quite clear, were connected to the important role she felt herself playing in the anthroposophical movement. Faced with the close working relationship and then the marriage of Rudolf Steiner and Marie von Sivers in the winter of 1914, Alice Sprengel not only sent personal letters to both but also brought her disappointment and sense of abandonment to the attention of other members of the Anthroposophical Society.

She also had a close relationship to Heinrich and Gertrud Goesch, a couple whose interest in Rudolf Steiner's work was matched by an equally strong fascination with the then emerging psychoanalytical school of Freud. Influenced by Alice Sprengel and his own inner uncertainties, Heinrich Goesch accused Rudolf Steiner both privately and publicly of manipulating the membership of the Anthroposophical Society into a dependent status. As supposed mechanisms of such manipulation he mentioned Steiner's repeated failure to keep appointments and physical contact with members through shaking hands upon meeting.

Rudolf Steiner was understandably upset by both sets of accusations and even more so by the gossiping and dissension they caused among members of the Anthroposophical Society. He used these difficulties as an opportunity to address four important questions that are as relevant today as they were in 1915. The first, primarily discussed in Lectures One and Two, concerns the nature of the Anthroposophical Society and the responsibilities its members have to accept if they want to be true to spiritual science. The very clear, pragmatic manner in which these two lectures discuss this important issue makes them a valuable companion to the recently published *The Christmas Conference for the Foundation of the Anthroposophical Society, 1923/24.*[1] The need for the members to move from a consumer orientation regarding spiritual teaching to a feeling of responsibility for it, the unique nature of the Anthroposophical Society as an earthly home for spiritual revelation, and the harm that irresponsible statements and actions can cause the Society are just a few of the important points covered. Steiner also takes a stand against the incessant gossiping and the mutual criticism among members as well as against their attempts to justify sexual infidelities by pointing to an incontrovertible "karma." Rudolf Steiner here urgently appeals to the members' sense of truth and exactitude as the basis for a healing and nurturing of the Anthroposophical Society.

The second question addressed, particularly in Lectures Three and Five, concerns the nature and conditions of spiritual seership. Steiner uses a discussion of Swedenborg's inability to understand the thoughts of certain spirit beings to make two fundamental points about spiritual cognition. The first is the difference between perception in the physical world and true spiritual seership. In the physical world we perceive objects outside of ourselves and take something of them into us

[1] Rudolf Steiner, *The Christmas Conference for the Foundation of the Anthroposophical Society, 1923/24* (Hudson, NY: Anthroposophic Press, 1990).

2

through mental images. In the spiritual world "we no longer perceive but experience that we are being perceived, that the spiritual beings of the higher hierarchies are observing us. This experience of being perceived and observed by the Angeloi and Archangeloi and other spiritual hierarchies is a total reversal of our former relationship to the physical world."[2]

According to Steiner, Swedenborg did not achieve this reversal of perspective; therefore, his clairvoyance was limited, and he did not attain to full imaginative cognition.

Steiner links this difference in perspectives to that between clairvoyance achieved through the redirection of sexual energies and clairvoyance resulting from pure thinking. The latter leads to the experience that the transformed thinking activity of the human being, a thinking devoid of personal likes and dislikes, allows thoughts to appear as objective entities within the human soul. It thereby properly prepares the individual for spiritual seership. The transformation of sexual energies, on the other hand, keeps the individual tied to the physical and allows only a partial clairvoyance. Steiner therefore contends that a spiritual science and seership appropriate to our time rests not on a transformation of our instincts but on a conscious separation of the instinctual life from that of the mind and spirit.

The third issue discussed by Rudolf Steiner in these lectures is the nature of psychoanalysis as developed by Freud. While acknowledging the importance of the unconscious and the subconscious, Steiner is particularly critical of the theory of infantile sexuality. It should be noted that Steiner gave these lectures in 1915 and that both Adler and Jung broke with Freud over Freud's insistence on infantile sexuality as a primary interpretive framework for understanding psychological disturbances.[3]

Freudian psychology is discussed in Lectures Four and Five of this volume. They are an important supplement to the

---

[2] See Lecture Three in this volume, pp. 43–44.
[3] See I. Progoff, *The Death and Rebirth of Psychology* (New York: McGraw Hill, 1973).

recently published lectures of Rudolf Steiner entitled *Psychoanalysis and Spiritual Psychology*.[4] Of particular significance is Rudolf Steiner's treatment of the three main physiological functions of the human being—the nerve sense system, the rhythmic system, and the metabolic system—in their historical and spiritual evolution. His insistence that the metabolic system and the instinctual sexual life are the least spiritual aspects of the human being supports both his criticism of Freud and his basic view of spiritual development.

In reading both these lectures and those contained in *Psychoanalysis and Spiritual Psychology*, one can easily be led to reject much of the development of psychology in the twentieth century. Indeed the anti-psychological orientation of many students of Rudolf Steiner's work is quite pronounced. My own perspective is different. First, I see the development of modern psychology and psychiatry as co-existent with the end of what Rudolf Steiner refers to as "the Kali Yuga," or dark age, in 1899. This means that however inadequate the evolution of psychological theories and practices has been in some respects, it has on the whole been a new and deepening exploration of the human soul and spirit. Here, I am in particular thinking of Jung in *Memories, Dreams, and Reflections* or of Viktor Frankl's logotherapy or Assagioli's work. It seems to me that while there is much in modern psychology that is trivial and dangerous, there is also much that is worthwhile and helpful.

Students of Rudolf Steiner's work have the possibility to ask questions of appropriateness and relevance regarding different psychological schools, as David Black has done in "On the Nature of Psychology" in *Towards*.[5] To see biophysical, behavioral, intrapsychic, and phenomenological schools of thought as addressing different levels of the human being, and to ask what spiritual science has to contribute to the evolving body of

[4] Rudolf Steiner, *Psychoanalysis and Spiritual Psychology* (Hudson, NY: Anthroposophic Press, 1990).
[5] *Towards*, 1 no. 7 (Winter 1980/81): 29–34.

psychological and spiritual insight in the last decade of the twentieth century, is a more honest and, I believe, more helpful approach than to extend Steiner's early opposition to Freud and Jung into an unreflecting anti-psychological stance. Soul work and spirit work are intimately connected. The task of developing a more spiritual psychology is a vital task for the coming decades.

In Lecture Six, Steiner addresses the relation between love, mysticism, and spirituality. Particularly significant is his contention that the prevailing materialism of the time made it impossible for most people to conceive of a spiritual striving that did not have some erotic or sexual basis, albeit a very refined one. While Rudolf Steiner does acknowledge that this is sometimes the case, he again asserts the importance of spiritual science as a path of spiritual development for Western humanity in our time because of its reliance on the transformation of the individual's thinking.

As this volume also contains all of the correspondence regarding the difficulties in the Anthroposophical Society in 1915, readers will easily see the direct connection between the personal accusations leveled against Steiner and the lecture themes presented. The questions raised are basic ones for any modern spiritual movement that wants to contribute to individual freedom and a renewal of society. These lectures can lead members of the Anthroposophical Society to ponder their responsibilities toward the content of spiritual science, toward Rudolf Steiner, and toward their brothers and sisters in their striving. For outside observers these lectures constitute an insightful record of the social and psychological difficulties of a spiritual movement relying primarily on the insights and teachings of one individual.

However, the questions of love, sexuality, morality, and spiritual development are of immediate interest and of deep personal significance for all readers on their inner journey.

Spring Valley, New York   CHRISTOPHER SCHAEFER, PH.D.
February 1991

PART ONE

Terms and Conditions of Life in the Anthroposophical Society

LECTURE ONE

Requirements of Our Life Together in the Anthroposophical Society

DORNACH, SEPTEMBER 10, 1915

MY DEAR FRIENDS! Movements such as our spiritual scientific movement have always been fostered in such a way that something that was to be impressed upon the spiritual culture of the times, or on culture in general, was first cultivated on the level of some formal social organization or society. And since the conditions of human interaction are the same today as they have been throughout history, it is also necessary for us, to a certain extent, to cultivate our spiritual scientific strivings within the framework of a formal organization.

Now, it has been the experience of almost all such organizations that it is difficult, at least in actual practice, to understand the concept of the society needed to foster a particular spiritual current like this. Time and again we're presented with evidence that there are very many people who actually do not like having to join a society. They admit that they feel uncomfortable about joining such a society; they would prefer to absorb its spiritual wealth through reading or listening to lectures not bound to any organized society, or through still other means. Only this morning, for example, I received a letter to that effect.

9

The kinds of reasons people give for taking this position have to be taken seriously. But let me emphasize again that a spiritual movement like this one is of necessity very different in its impulses and its whole way of thinking, feeling, and doing from the thinking, feeling, and doing of the other people around it. Therefore, to introduce such a movement to humanity with no help from a formal organization would be much more difficult than to do this by means of a society whose members are preparing, through their interactions and their ongoing absorption of spiritual scientific thoughts and concepts, to be a kind of tool or instrument for disseminating our spiritual science. As a consequence, however, the concept of a society of this kind has to be taken extremely seriously, because in quite practical terms this society has to become a vehicle for the spiritual current in question.

You need only look at our own Society as an example and examine how different it is from other societies, associations, or organizations that people have called into existence. This difference will be particularly noticeable if you keep one thing in mind. Just suppose that recent events confronting us had made us entertain the thought of disbanding the Anthroposophical Society as such. Let's assume hypothetically that we wanted to dissolve the Society because of problems within it. Now, if the Anthroposophical Society were simply an organization like many others, of course it would be possible to simply dissolve it, set something else up in its place, and eliminate the disgraceful circumstances in the process.

However, our Anthroposophical Society is different in a very significant respect from other organizations or societies founded on the basis of some program with a certain number of points and statutes. That kind of society can be dissolved at any moment. If we were to dissolve the Anthroposophical Society, however, it would not be dissolved in actual fact. As the Anthroposophical Society, as a society existing on behalf of a spiritual scientific movement, we are different from other societies

10

in that our Society is founded, not on a program of abstract and therefore unreal points, but on something very real. Our basis is a real one.

Just look at the fact that each member of the Anthroposophical Society is entitled to have access to our lecture cycles, while other people are not.[1] That's a very real basis, because dissolving the Anthroposophical Society would do so in name only; it would not do away with the fact that a certain number of people are in possession of these cycles. And it is an equally real fact that a certain number of people are carrying a specific wealth of wisdom in their heads. I cannot tell exactly how great the percentage is of people who have the things we talk about in their heads—in contrast to those who only have them in "visions"—but that's not the important thing as far as the Society is concerned. It remains a reality that a certain wealth of wisdom, a sum total of things that really exist, are present in the hearts and minds of people who have belonged to the Anthroposophical Society until now. That cannot be taken away from them even by dissolving the Society.

So the Anthroposophical Society is different from other societies in that it will not tolerate any figments of the imagination in its organization, but is constructed on the basis of reality. Thus, dissolving it would have absolutely no immediate effect on its continued existence as far as reality is concerned. Our Society compares to other societies and organizations as something real compares to things that are merely thought out. We must keep this weighty difference in mind in order to understand the concept of our Society in the right way. And it is only because a large number of members have counted, more or less consciously, on our Society's solid grounding in reality, on its basis in something more than programmatic points, that we see an institute of higher learning for spiritual science being built on this hill, a building that will further enhance our connection to something real.

It would be possible for some group of dreamers to get

11

together and decide not to wear collars and ties, to wear only sandals on their feet, and perhaps to simplify life in other ways by disregarding certain other social conventions or "prejudices," as they might call them. (I have chosen a hypothetical example so that no one present needs to feel put on the spot.) Disbanding a group like that would not change anything significant. But we are not simply a group of dreamers; we are different in that we are fully aware of the weight and importance of our grounding in reality.

Without getting into splitting hairs, we also need to distinguish between the concept of a society such as the one in which we develop a specific spiritual teaching, and that of a club or similar organization. We have to admit that the appropriate concept of a such a society eludes many of us when we think about the conditions of our life in this Society, and we are left contemplating the concept of a club or similar organization. In that kind of organization, statutes and conditions are set up that have to be met. In a Society like ours, however, that is not enough. It is different from a club in much more than name only.

In our Society, the important thing, as I have explained several times in the last few weeks, is that the concept of the society really be taken seriously.[2] This means that all members must be aware that belonging to the Society involves more than simply receiving membership cards and being entitled to call themselves members of the Society. In fact, they are all organs of the Society. Because of that, something subtle and yet very specific has to live among the members, something for which each member should feel a certain responsibility. As individuals, they must be aware of both the obvious and subtler needs and well-being of other members of the Society, and experienced members must be ready and willing to use their experience in supporting those who have joined more recently. These more experienced members do not necessarily have to reveal their experience; after all, what matters is how they apply their experience in daily life.

The word "trust" often comes up in this connection. In the course of a lecture I gave a few weeks ago, I explained that we do not need to have trust in our teachings, because these teachings will try to justify our confidence in them through every single practical measure they give rise to.[3] However, we do need to try to have trust in each other and to make sure that trust is justified. We must try to bring about real connections between members. It goes a long way toward developing the kind of "ideal aura" necessary in a Society such as ours if each experienced member, without snooping around like a spy or a detective—that is, without violating anyone's privacy—can really keep an eye on the ups and downs of only ten other members, and do it without having to tell them they are considered less experienced. Of course, it's impossible to legislate trust; it has to be earned. Our more experienced members need to make a concerted effort to win the trust of those who have been in the Society for only a short time.

Such things have been mentioned often in the course of our Society's years of activity, but it has never been as necessary to speak about them as it is here and now. When members of the Anthroposophical Society were scattered among the rest of the population in various cities, that was a very different state of affairs from so many of us living here on top of each other, on display for everyone else, so to speak. This situation makes it imperative that we take a long and serious look at the basic premises of how we live together in the Society.

Of course, a society such as ours will never be able to please all the people living outside it. It will never be able to prevent some of these people from indulging in all kinds of slander, ridicule, unjustified attacks, and so on. But that's not the point; what I am going to say now is independent of all that. The important thing is that the members of the Society really do everything possible in each single instance to show up the attacks as unjustified and lacking any basis in fact. To do this, we have to look at details, my friends. It's not enough to just pay attention to the major issues in our outer life. We have to be equally aware of the little things.

For instance, if some of our members are sitting among other people on the trolley on the way back to Basel at night, and they talk loudly about every little twinge in their ether body, that is not exactly a crime. If someone criticizes them for it, we might well reply, "So what? Is it all that important?" In fact, however, it is really very important because it puts the dignity and seriousness of our movement in question. Thus, even though such incidents are only trifling matters, they ought to be avoided. We ought to start reforming ourselves wherever that change can have a real effect. Above all, we have to realize that when we talk in front of other people about things only we can understand, those people will not be able to avoid getting wrong impressions.

We can assume that we know what we are talking about when we speak about the ether body, but the people who may be listening do not. They may be in the same situation as a maid whom some of my closer acquaintances know well. This woman worked for anthroposophists, and because she was interested in finding out what anthroposophy was all about, she attended an introductory course given by one of our members, and came home saying, "Well, I learned that I have four bodies, not just one. But I have this tiny little room and a very narrow bed, and now I don't know how all those bodies are going to fit in!" This is a true story. It took place in the house of people I know quite well. So you see, people who hear you talking about all the little twinges of your ether body will naturally think that you're talking about the ether body as if it were a physical body; thus, you are actually leading them astray and keeping them from developing any closer connection to our movement.

That's why it is important for us to learn to take the things we talk about seriously and precisely. Even if they are only minor matters in themselves, they can raise a virtual wall of prejudices around us, and that can and should be avoided. In a society like this, it is important for us to learn to speak really precisely, or else it may gradually become impossible to foster what should be fostered within this Society.

Today I feel compelled to mention a number of things that will probably seem totally superfluous to most of you, simply because the natural response is, "Well, what is that supposed to mean—we need to be precise in our way of speaking? Of course we do." But just keep your eyes and ears open next time something happens somewhere or other, when something has been said and one person passes it on to the next. If you really pay close attention to whether or not things are being presented accurately, in many instances you will easily notice the deviation from what is strictly accurate. When something someone has heard or seen gets passed on to the next person and then to the next, and so on, what comes out can be a monstrous caricature of what actually happened or was actually said. This experience is all too common in our Society.

We have to take into account that, in a spiritual scientific movement, we can work constructively only if we get used to being exact, to really understanding things precisely. Spiritual science forces us to focus spiritually on things that have nothing to do with the outer physical world, and in order to develop the right relationship to them, we need a counterbalance of some kind. The only suitable counterbalance is to approach things on the physical plane as realistically as possible. After all, accuracy belongs to reality.

Some time ago I gave a public lecture in Munich that really startled a number of people.[4] Its subject was the nature of evil. In that lecture, I explained that the forces at work in evil on the physical plane are in a sense nothing else but forces that have been transferred from higher planes of existence to the physical plane. Certain forces that can lead us to recognize and master the spiritual if applied up there in the spiritual world can turn to evil down here in the physical world.

The force that enables us to understand the spiritual world belongs only in the spiritual world; this same force causes all kinds of harm if it is directly and thoughtlessly transferred to the physical plane. For what is the nature of this force? It consists in making one's thinking independent of the physical plane. When this capacity is applied to the physical plane itself, it turns into deceit and dishonesty. Thus, people who were called upon to disseminate spiritual science have always seen great danger in doing so, because what is needed for understanding higher planes of existence is harmful when applied directly to the physical world.

That is why a counterbalance is needed: in order to keep our ability to understand the spiritual world suitably pure and beautiful, we must develop our feeling for truth and exactitude in the physical world as thoroughly as possible. If we do not count on exactitude on the physical plane, then in a so-called occult society certain tendencies developed through spiritual scientific practices immediately mingle inappropriately with the very lowest aspects of the physical plane.

Let's look at ordinary materialistic society in a broader sense of the word. As you know—or you may have heard about it even if you have no firsthand knowledge of it—there are certain social circles where gossip prevails. At least from hearsay, you will be aware that this gossip or tittle-tattle is going on, that it prevails in ordinary materialistic bourgeois society. The quality of this gossip is usually not very high and much can be said against it, but at least for the most part no esoteric contents get mixed up with it. But when gossip is the general rule in an occult society, esoteric ideas are the first to get drawn into it.

I hope it is possible to really talk about things like this in our circle, because it should be possible to say something within our Society without having it immediately spread abroad in places where it is then misunderstood. Our experiences in this regard,

16

however, are also not the best, and if they continue, we will indeed have to organize our Society differently. Things that are said within the Society have to remain in the Society in the strictest sense of the word, because it really must be possible from time to time to say things that could not simply be said casually outside our Society.

Of course, in our Society we often have to talk about the karmic relationships between people. It may well be that such relationships exist—in fact, of course they exist—but if we continually get our views on karma mixed up with our ordinary everyday relationships, we are not taking the concept of truthfulness literally enough, and the result is not only nonsensical but also harmful. Truthfulness is a concept that has to be applied extremely strictly.

I can think of any number of cases in esoteric circles, both inside and outside our Society, where subjective matters that take place as a matter of course on the physical plane have been studded and embellished with esoteric truths. Let me mention one extreme example that may not happen very frequently in our Society, but it is one of the things that can be experienced. Indeed, it has happened numerous times.

Many people have learned about reincarnation, and they have also learned that Christ was alive on Earth at a certain point in time. I have experienced more than once that women who have become aware of these two spiritual facts—reincarnation and Christ's incarnation—have in all seriousness imagined that they have been chosen to give birth to the Christ and have attempted to arrange their lives to make this possible. It is unpleasant to have to mention these things and call a spade a spade, but we must do it to protect the Society, which we can do only if we don't close our eyes to the harm people can cause by applying occult truths on the physical plane.

Granted, the case I just mentioned is extreme, but it has happened not only once, but over and over again. I have described it drastically because things like this happen very frequently on

17

a smaller scale, and it is important to notice the minor instances as well as the more blatant ones. Of course, it is a major issue if someone thinks she is going to give birth to the Christ, because the consequences can be extremely unfortunate. On a smaller scale, however, things like this are happening again and again.

Now, in ordinary bourgeois life, it happens that people fall in love, that a man falls in love with a woman. People simply call it "falling in love," and that's the plain and simple truth. In esoteric societies men and women also fall in love; the possibility cannot be ruled out, as some of you know from experience. But in that case, what you hear about it is not as simple as, "X has fallen in love with Y." Ordinary people just say that they're going together, which is usually a very accurate description as outward observation goes. But in esoteric societies, what you hear about it often goes something like this: "Having thoroughly examined my karma, I find that another personality has entered it, and we have realized that karma has destined us to be with each other and to intervene in the destiny of the world in a particular way."

People fail to notice how much deception has crept in between this assertion and the simple matter of falling in love. This deception has developed in the following way: In bourgeois materialistic society, it's considered quite normal for two people to fall in love. But in an esoteric society, this is often not considered normal; instead, it is something people feel slightly ashamed of. But people do not like to feel ashamed. We don't need to go into why that is the case; there can be any number of reasons. People simply do not like to feel ashamed, so instead, they say that karma has spoken and has to be obeyed. Of course they are not acting out of pure selfishness or pure emotion—far from it; karma has to be obeyed! But if they were truthful, they would just admit that they have fallen in love, and having admitted it, they would find their way through life much more readily than by getting the truth mixed up with all kinds of karmic nonsense. The basic mischief of embellishing personal matters with esoteric truths leads to ever greater harm because it makes people lose their inner sense of limits, the limits we have to accept when we adopt a spiritual scientific philosophy.

This is not to say that we should introduce the worst principles of uncultured circles into our Society. In certain social circles, it is said that being human begins with being a baron. We must not establish our own version of this by saying that being human begins with being either a spiritual scientist or an anthroposophist—with being an "anthropop," as others are starting to call it. We must not do that. We have to admit that even before we became spiritual scientists, we were people with certain ways of looking at things, people who would have done certain things and abstained from others.

In the very early days of our movement, I pointed out how important it is that we do not use our spiritual scientific views to sink down below our earlier level of moral standards, but that we must rise above it in all respects. That is why I said many years ago that when we entered the Society, each of us was equipped with a certain stock of moral standards and habitual ways of doing things, and that we should allow these habits to remain as they are until some clear and incontrovertible inner necessity compels us to change them. Generally, this happens only much later on. It can be extremely detrimental if, after having learned a little bit from spiritual science, we take what we have learned and use it to excuse or embellish what we do in life. You have to be perfectly clear on one point, my friends, namely that the outer circumstances of our life also come about through karma of a certain kind. And how people out in the world think and act is also a matter of karma.

Now, as you know, I prefer to talk about concrete cases because they are the most telling. For example, the following once happened to me: Not long ago, I was sitting in a barber shop— excuse me for talking about things like this, but what I'm going to tell you is not all that indiscreet or intimate. I was sitting in front of the mirror, so I could see the people as they came and went. The door opened, and in came a man who had on some kind of shoes that were nothing more than pieces of soft leather tied together; above that, he was wearing leggings and some kind of capelike garment draped at a coquettish angle. In addition, his hair was swept back with some kind of a headband. Coincidentally, as it were, I knew the man very well.[5]

The barber let go of the razor he had just started to apply to my face and bought something from the man for five pennies. He showed it to me once the man had gone out—it was a poem he had composed himself. It was a simply terrible poem, but that man was going around the streets and stores in that get-up, selling the thing and imagining himself to be infinitely superior to all the people around him. He thought he was following some great ideal, but in reality he was only following an exaggerated and hysterical form of vanity. The basic impulse behind his conduct, his whole way of being, was nothing more than a gross exaggeration of the principle at work among the vainest and most superficial ladies.

But just consider how many among us might once have been tempted—for courtesy's sake, I will not suggest that they might still be tempted today—to say that in his own way, that man was only trying to do the right thing. True enough, but it was still absolute and total nonsense, and bound to make a mess of a person's life if he made it the principle of a lifetime. We have to realize to what extent vanity can be a motivating factor in what people do, and how difficult it is to notice it. If we take seriously what we can gain from spiritual science and accept it with respect, we have to admit that vanity is a very strong force in that man. If we do something or other out of vanity, not to mention other drives and impulses, other people are offended, though not necessarily for the reasons we might suspect. Nonetheless, there is a connection between ourselves and what other people say about us, a connection that is very easy to find if we look carefully. And we can only get beyond things like that if we develop a strict sense of exactitude as a counterbalance, an attitude we also need for understanding esoteric truths. Although it's only a detail and no major issue, in esotericism it is extremely important to know and to observe, when people are recounting things, whether they are recounting their own observations and thus have a right to be talking about them as facts, or whether they are passing on things they heard from someone else. We must be able to tell the difference. But in hundreds of cases, people say things to others who in turn tell someone else, but in such a way that the person third in line gets the impression that they are not simply passing on something they've heard, but are talking about their own direct experience and have a right to be talking about it as if it were actual fact. This lack of precision is less important in ordinary materialistic society than it is among us. In materialistic circles, it may be pedantic to be so precise in how one speaks, but in our Society, more so than anywhere else, we need to observe such things strictly and exactly. And above all, we need to make a practice of being precise about ourselves.

If any of you need to be convinced of the implications of what I am saying, you are welcome to make the following experiment: Choose some topic—vegetarianism, for example—and observe how certain adherents of spiritual science talk about this topic in the outside world. Make a chart, and each time you hear spiritual scientists telling other people that they are vegetarians, jot down the reasons they give. It will soon become clear that on the subject of vegetarianism, adherents of spiritual science often say absolutely scandalous things to people in the outside world. When the outside world then comes to the conclusion that we are a society of fools, it should come as no great surprise.

In anthroposophical circles, I have frequently mentioned a very simple way of responding to the question of why you are a vegetarian without antagonizing people around you. If someone asks why you are a vegetarian, and you know that person would never eat horsemeat, you simply respond with the question, "Well, why don't you eat horsemeat?" Now the two of you are on the same footing, and the person who has to give a reason for not eating horsemeat will probably not come up with any highly theoretical reasons, but will say something like "The thought of it makes me sick." Then you can say, "That's just how any meat makes me feel." And as long as you say this in an appropriately conciliatory way, people will understand your point of view. The main thing is not to let the other person get the impression that you feel superior because of not eating meat. You might still want to add, although only if you can honestly admit it to yourself, that you are too weak to eat meat; you're handicapped when it comes to eating meat. When this question has come up, I myself have often said that a lot of things are simply easier to get through if you don't eat meat. Meat weighs people down, and if you need to use your brain in a precise way, it is simply easier to do if you don't eat meat. In the end, it all comes down to the question of what is easier and more convenient.

I have often emphasized that it is impossible to eat your way into the higher worlds, either through what you eat or through what you abstain from eating. Achieving access to spiritual worlds is a spiritual matter, and both eating and abstaining from food are physical matters. If this were not the case, people might get grotesque ideas about what would happen if they did or did not eat certain foods. It might occur to them to eat salt one week and no salt at all the next week in order to descend to the depths of the elemental world during the week when they were eating salt and come back up again in the course of the week when they were doing without. It's quite possible for people to get stupid ideas like that. In our Society, of course, people will not get ideas that are as stupid as that, but similar things might still occur to them.

But to get back to the subject of vegetarianism, if we are as modest as possible in how we discuss it in the presence of outsiders, we will find that eventually no one will hold the fact that we are vegetarians against us. On the other hand, if we consider vegetarianism to be something to our credit, the outside world will never forgive us for it. And in fact, being vegetarian is not a credit to anyone; it is simply an easy way out.

There are many other similar examples, and we really have to talk about things like this, not to preach morality, but to establish certain basic principles for our life in an esoteric society vis-à-vis the outside world. What it all comes down to is that we need to seriously consider how we relate to the outside world, and the result of our deliberations must be both a bridge and a protective wall between us and the outside, especially in the case of a society like ours. It happens again and again, for instance, that members say to people on the outside, "Dr. Steiner said this and such." Just put yourself in the place of the person you're talking to, and imagine what it feels like!

For example, if someone says that Dr. Steiner is taking so-and-so's spiritual development in hand, how are outsiders supposed to understand that? What can they possibly imagine except a society of fools who all subordinate themselves to a single individual? That kind of thing really does happen. I cannot even pretend that it does not occur. And just imagine what it means to the outside world. We really must talk about these things from the point of view of how a society should be set up if a spiritual scientific movement like ours is to inhabit it. First and foremost, we must take this spiritual scientific movement seriously, and we must not do anything that could be detrimental to it in the eyes of the outside world.

I will go into this subject more deeply tomorrow, and you will see how intimately this all relates to certain specific impulses of spiritual science. I do not want to simply lecture you sternly; I want to explain how these things relate to the central impulses of spiritual science.

The Anthroposophical Society
as a Living Being

DORNACH, SEPTEMBER 11, 1915

YESTERDAY, my dear friends, I explained the primary difference between a society like ours and other societies or associations. I said its statutes and the points on its program do not exhaustively describe the character of our Society—if we add or delete points and statutes, nothing significant will be added to or subtracted from what our Society is essentially meant to be. I also pointed out the most obvious way in which our Society differs from the usual kind of program-based society or association. That kind of association can be dissolved at any moment. But if it became necessary to dissolve our Society and we actually disbanded, that would in no way change the real state of affairs since our Society, unlike others, is based not on illusory human inventions such as programs and statutes, but on realities. We touched on one of these realities, namely that the lecture cycles are in the hands of all our members, a fact that would not change in the slightest if the Society were dissolved. And the same applies to many other realities on which our Society is based.

Consequently, we really must get to know the conditions necessary for the survival of our Society and not delude ourselves about them. I gave a rather superficial explanation of these conditions yesterday, and would like to go into them more deeply today.

You all know that in many materialistic discussions on the nature of life itself, we can find many definitions or explanations of what constitutes a living being. You have probably learned enough on that subject from spiritual science to realize that all these explanations and definitions are of necessity one-sided and incomplete. The greatest mistake or illusion of materialistically minded people is to think they can encompass the essence of a thing in a single definition or explanation. To illustrate how grotesque this idea is, I once told you the story of how a Greek school of philosophy was searching for a definition of the human being. What they finally came up with was that a human being was a living being with two legs and no feathers.[1] Well, this is undoubtedly correct; it is an absolutely correct definition. But the next day, someone who had understood this definition brought in a plucked chicken and said, "Here is a living thing that has two legs and no feathers, so it must be a human being!"

The usual attempts at defining life are no better than that. That's just the way it is with definitions, and we have to be aware of that fact. There is also a comparable materialistic definition of life given by a famous zoologist, a definition that is quite correct and useful within the limits of its applicability:[2] "A living thing is something that can leave a corpse behind under certain circumstances; what it leaves behind when it is destroyed is thus not a living thing." Clearly, this definition applies only to the outer limits of the physical plane, where a living being does in fact leave a corpse behind at its demise; thus, this definition is valid there. When a machine is destroyed, it does not leave a corpse behind; we would be speaking metaphorically if we talked about the corpse of a watch, for instance. However, if our Society were dissolved, it would actually leave behind a real corpse, in the truest sense of the word.

What is the nature of a corpse? Once a corpse has been abandoned by its soul, it no longer obeys the same laws as it did when it was united with that soul. Instead, it begins to obey the physical laws of the earthly elements. The same thing would be true of the corpse of our Society as soon as the Society was dissolved. In addition, the Society's vehicle, namely all the lecture cycles now in the members' possession, would also be part of this corpse.

We can be quite precise and scientific in taking this comparison further. If a corpse is not to have a detrimental effect on its surroundings, it must be cremated or buried. This would also apply to the corpse our Society would undoubtedly leave behind at its dissolution. As a consequence, once we know what our Society really is, we become aware of our responsibility toward what it is based on. A society or association based on statutes and programs is like a machine that leaves behind only pieces if you destroy it, but our Society would leave an actual corpse behind if it were dissolved. It would leave behind something that would have to be thought of as a corpse and treated accordingly.

My friends, we really must think about what our Society requires to survive. For the time being, let's turn away from the superficial fact that the lecture cycles exist and look at their content, which, as I mentioned yesterday, is now present in a certain number of heads. It exists not only in the heads of people who took it in properly and harmoniously, but perhaps also of those—present company excepted, of course, for politeness' sake—who took it up in a distorted form and go on distorting it as they talk about it. All of this is really there and is alive in the Society. And just think of the effect it would have as the Society's corpse if the Society were to disband. That is why we must take responsibility for guarding what our Society requires for survival, and why I appealed to you yesterday in various ways to safeguard those needs.

Now, I just said that if the Society were dissolved, it would leave behind a corpse. This characteristic tells us that in the truest sense of the word, the Society is a real living being. But the Society also possesses another characteristic of living things, namely the fact that it can get sick. I told you that an association founded on the basis of a program and statutes is like a machine or a mechanism, and when members do something that does not fit in with the machine, they are expelled. Expelling members from an association founded on statutes is always just a matter of "lovingly" applying a rule.

However, in the case of a society like ours, which is a living organism rather than a mechanism, taking the action of expelling a member will very seldom have any significant effect on the actual problem. In our circumstances, expelling a member who has done something wrong is simply taking the easy way out. That is not to say that we cannot do it, but we do have to realize that it is much more important to keep the organism of our Society so healthy that it acts as a healer in its totality when confronted with individual unhealthy growths. In most cases, healing a sick organism is nothing more than calling up the healing forces of the entire organism when an individual member or organ is ill. It is important that we understand the process of potential illness within our Society and become aware of the need to call up the healing forces of its entire organism.

Now, I already explained yesterday that one important force for healing consists in getting used to being absolutely exact with regard to phenomena on the physical plane—truth in exactitude, and exactitude in truthfulness. In outer exoteric life, if some bit of information is altered through gossip or lack of precision in being passed on from one person to the next, that doesn't matter nearly as much as it would matter if we were to let this become habitual within our Society. One of the most urgent needs, then, is for us to take exactitude as our guiding principle in everything we say and do.

It is only natural for people to ask what they must do in order to help strengthen the Society. The answer is that the single most important thing is for each individual to really feel like a member of the Society in the right way. Members must experience the Society as an organism and themselves as its organs. That requires, however, that we all make the affairs of the Society our own and that we are able to follow the Society's train of thought. Knowing about the concerns of the Society and wanting to know about them is of fundamental, crucial importance. Of course, this presupposes a certain interest in the Society as such, and to develop this interest, we have to know that the Society is an organism and take this fact seriously. It is much more than just a metaphor.

For example, we need to understand the following. We have three points listed in our statutes.[3] It follows from what I said before that statutes are only of secondary importance for us. Nonetheless, they are there. In fact, they have to be there. And if we consider these three statutory points, we can describe them best by saying that they represent our work, the work of our Society. But if you think about how it is with human beings and their relationship to their work, you will find that people's work is what makes them tired and wears them out. Describing a person's work, however, by no means definitively characterizes that person, and it makes just as little sense to say that the work within the confines of these three points on our program encompasses the whole nature and essence of our Society.

However, performing this work does wear the Society down. This means that our Society, just like a human being, needs to be taken care of. Just like a human organism, the organism of the Society also needs care. And it's not enough to think that being a member of the Society means nothing more than using the Society as a place for fostering what is expressed in these three points in our statutes. It also means taking an interest in the guidance and management of the Society as such. When someone lacks this interest, that really means that person is opposed to the Society's ongoing existence. Being interested only in the work the Society does is not the same thing as being interested in the Society as such. But in order for our Society to exist as a basis for this work, a certain interest in the Society as such, in the Society as an organism, must also be present. That is, a certain principle of togetherness, of living and working together, has to be cultivated within our Society.

I said yesterday that in certain cases it is necessary to become quite drastic in calling a spade a spade, and also that it belongs to the very nature of our Society to be able to count on not having these things spread abroad immediately. The grotesque example I used yesterday, the example of the man in the barbershop whose habits were at odds with those of his surroundings, was meant to show that the motive behind this kind of clash is often quite different from what people claim. As I showed, the man in question was motivated by hysterical vanity.

Karma has led us to set up our headquarters here in this area, and so we find ourselves living under conditions that are not exactly ideal in all respects, if I may put it like that. That was what I meant when I said that even if each of us behaved in an absolutely exemplary manner, we might be attacked with still more slander and so on, even if all our members were absolutely exemplary in how they behaved within the general population. So you see, I am not saying that we must take all possible prejudices into account, but only that we need to look at the living conditions our Society needs.

In terms of our own human nature, our own physical body, we know that we have to be physically adapted to the external conditions of life around us, on which we depend, and that our physical organism is in constant interaction with the outside world. The same thing applies to the outer organism of our Society. It has to develop within the social framework in which our karma has placed us, and this makes it imperative that our members respect our Society's needs with regard to living conditions. I have explained what these conditions are time and time again.

An important point I once expressly stated in a rebuttal[4] of a local pastor's article attacking our Society[5] was that our Society as such does not have anything directly to do with religion. After all, what matters is not only to always say the right thing, but also to say what needs to be said in each particular instance. That is what is important. And one of the things most crucially needed for our whole movement to flourish is for the outer world to finally realize something I've tried to explain again and again. I have said repeatedly that our movement has no more to do with religion than the Copernican view of the solar system at its inception had to do with any particular religious confession. That the religious denominations were opposed to the Copernican system was their problem, and no reflection on the Copernican view itself. And now we must stand firm on one point, namely, that we have no intention of founding a sect or a religious movement. At one point, I had to get downright unpleasant, because, with the best will in the world, people were writing articles about our building and calling it a "temple," which was very detrimental to us. It made it seem, quite unnecessarily, as if we were competing with the religious denominations. That is why I always remind our members to try to popularize the term "School for Spiritual Science."

It is really important for people to hear again and again that we have nothing to do with a religious sect or with founding a new religion or anything like that. Our members commit untold sins against the Society when they fail to point out, when providing information, that our Society has nothing to do with founding a religion. Not only that, but by omission they actually do a lot to make it seem as if we were trying to found a religion. It is important to take this into account even in trivial instances and to take every opportunity to beat it into people's hard heads that this is not a temple and not a church, but something that is dedicated to scientific purposes.

Sometimes, my friends, what is said is less important than how it is said. We have to realize that we will always give outsiders the impression that we are a sect or some kind of new religion if we invariably put on a long face in talking about anything happening in our movement—"so long a face that your chin hits your stomach," as someone once put it to me.[6] I know this is not a nice way of putting it, but it is certainly to the point. Of course, this is because many people imagine that this kind of exaggerated seriousness is the only way to talk about feelings related to religious life. But we must make every effort to free our movement from the preconceived idea that we are trying to found a church, a religion, or a sect, and to popularize the idea that this is a spiritual scientific movement taking its place in the world just as the Copernican system did, so that everyone can see that we are the ones being wronged. The Church made a mistake in opposing the teachings of Copernicus; it had to accept them eventually anyway.[7] The same thing will happen with our movement as well—the Church will have to accept it.

This is an example of how we have to learn to speak very exactly, and precise speaking must be considered the lifeblood of our Society in its relations with the outside world. It is one way of doing something really constructive on behalf of the Society. People who are only interested in reading lecture cycles—which has its uses, of course, and we couldn't do without it—and take no interest in the governance of the Society, especially here, where you are all in such close contact—well, people who do not want to develop that interest are actually not in support of the Society as such, as I said before. You must develop an interest in the Society! The point is not simply to be there for the sake of participating somehow in the work the Society has to do, but to develop an interest in the Society as

31

such. This means, however, that the affairs of the Society as a living entity have to enter our individual awareness. And the less we need statutes in order to do that, the better.

You see how necessary it is for us to become more and more able to stand firm when someone from the outside says something negative about our Society, and to be able to say that we can vouch for the fact that something like that could not possibly happen in our Society. We must be able to count on the fact that the kind of slander that gets circulated is false in almost all instances—although exceptions are always possible, of course. This, however, requires a really vital interest in the affairs of the Society.

Let's assume that some kind of indiscretion occurs. For example, let's take the hypothetical case of a man and a woman who, one fine afternoon in May, are so indiscreet as to do something they shouldn't do, outside and in full view of the people in the neighborhood. Let's assume that this kind of indiscretion takes place. What ought to happen as a matter of course if our Society were constituted as it should be? The natural thing would be for the people in question to realize in the course of the next few days that they ought to find an older member in whom they could confide, and ask what can be done about it. That would mean that they are making their own private matters the concern of the Society.

Please note the kind of example I have chosen. It is not simply the kind of thing we should regard as a strictly private matter that is none of our business. Rather, it is something that could be extremely damaging to the Society. We cannot function on the principle of the knee that says, "That's my private business"; the knee has to feel like a part of the whole organism. Of course, such things must also be received with real interest. They have to be seen as a concern of the Society; there must always be someone there who is aware of not only what is of immediate interest to him or her, but who also knows a lot about the Society and can contribute to the Society's ongoing well-being.

In other words, this means that we have to get beyond saying, "I have my own circle of friends, and it's to my credit that I brought them into the Society; this circle of friends is what interests me." I certainly do not mean to criticize people for developing friendships and personal connections—that is none of the Society's business. However, it does have an immediate effect on the Society if people are only interested in the Society because of their own membership in it. We have to make the concerns of the Society our own. We must preclude the possibility of first hearing about some offensive incident from someone outside the Society rather than from within our own membership, and we will automatically take a step toward preventing this when the right kind of interest in our internal social relationships is present.

For instance, at present you can ask four or five people whether a particular person has been attending our lectures in the past few weeks, and discover that none of them knows. That can easily happen among us. Of course, it is understandable if one or the other person doesn't know anything about it, but if you cannot find out anything at all, even by asking around among people who can be presumed to be in the know, that demonstrates a lack of interest and shows that our Society is a mechanism, not an organism. It shows that people are not taking an interest in its life and vitality. That is what I want to emphasize again and again—the need for an interest in our Society's life and vitality.

You see, my friends, we are sometimes surprised by events in our Society that would not surprise us if the members were sensitive to their obligations—and I use that word deliberately—and were participating in the thinking, feeling, and doing of the Society as if they were part of a living organism. But two things are necessary for that to happen. First, each one of us must be willing not to deal with incidents touching on the Society's needs as if they were his or her strictly private concerns. And second, anyone willing to do that must seek out another member with a sympathetic ear.

In this present crisis involving the part of the Society around the building in Dornach, regardless of how many formal resolutions and new paragraphs you formulate, you will still not be able to cope with what is going on in the Society. In spite of all that, we will still not be able to prevent ending up with the above-mentioned corpse on our hands. You can only prevent it by beginning to take an active interest in the affairs of the Society. This means more than the one-time application of intelligence and good sense to formulating new paragraphs and setting up tribunals to deal with "transgressions"; it means making the Society an ongoing object of interest in a living context. But above all, it means we must not be afraid to think, regardless of how unsettling that may be.

I have already mentioned that we are now living in a highly abnormal phase of European history, which we hope will soon come to an end. In times like this, we have to realize that we should not feel free to send anything and everything we happen to think of over international borders, even if it is nothing incorrect or offensive. I am not talking about private matters, I'm talking about things that concern the Society. In fact, however, a large number of our members do not want to think at all about what might or might not be appropriate to the times. Of course, nothing wrong has been done and I do not mean to reprimand anyone, but only to encourage you all to give it some thought and consideration before you act.

We all know that applications for membership or notices of acceptance are totally innocuous documents that cannot possibly cause political repercussions. However, that is not how nations at war look at things. So why do our members insist on sending membership cards out of the country? Perhaps out of thoughtlessness, perhaps out of stubbornness, because they have a point to prove. But if such things continue to happen on a large scale, people will mistakenly read all kinds of things into them, and it will become impossible for the Society to continue to exist. Our members, of all people, ought to be distinguished by their ability to think! But we have to pay attention to these things, or we will not see the Society continue for very much longer.

Once in a while I need to refer back to things in the past. For example, our criterion for admitting members to the Society has never been that only exceptional human beings who were head and shoulders above the rest of humanity would be considered. That is what many people think, but it's not true, and there are others who think that people who are admitted to the Society are in no way exceptional. In fact, we also made a point of admitting people to help them become healthy. And then what happened? Other members began to regard one of these people, someone who was to be helped by being admitted, as a kind of apostle, as someone who was there to heal the Society.

Why is it possible, my friends, for something like that to happen? It is because we are not adequately aware of the ways and means we have at our disposal to prevent it. Just think back to some of the things that have happened—and think we must, if we are to sustain an esoteric movement! If you think back, you will find that whenever something like that happened, whatever you needed in order to be able to assess the situation was usually made available in a lecture; it was spoken out. You only had to be alert to it whenever some danger was present. This means, however, that you really have to consider in detail the lectures given during the time in question. There is no need for us to make the mistake of getting overly personal in our efforts to do the right thing; we can stick to objective facts. But we have to understand what is objectively true on a case-by-case basis.

At this point, there can be no doubt that something radical and fundamental has to happen, especially for that part of our Society gathered around this building. But it is high time to make sure that we do not look for this fundamental and radical action in the wrong direction, that we do not believe it can be accomplished through a few simple things, a few principles and resolutions. That will not bring about any fundamental change or any fundamental healing.

My friends, I must confess that it is not at all easy for me to discuss these things as I have been doing yesterday and today, simply because I would prefer to be talking about other things, of course, and because I also know that many of you have no desire to hear such things, since, after all, your reason for being here is to hear various esoteric truths. However, my friends, if the Society continues to be of as little use as the recent actions of some individuals suggest, we may have to concede that it is no longer possible to use it as a vehicle for introducing spiritual science into the world. Just think of the discrepancy between what I have just said and something else I have had to say here many times in the last few weeks, namely, that spiritual science as we know it must be the greatest influence of our times in counteracting the presumptuous, superficial, and deceptive knowledge existing in the name of science and research. Indeed, spiritual science must make itself felt as a fundamentally progressive element within humankind. And yet we still have to talk about things that should really be self-explanatory, and all this at the risk of being constantly misunderstood. We all tend to see the sins of the other and not make the effort to see our Society as a real living organism, that is, to experience ourselves as organs within this organism.

Of course, members who have joined us only recently can easily make mistakes, but I wonder what some of the long-term members are doing here if they are not doing anything to prevent the mistakes of the newcomers. It should be a principle of ours that longtime members pay attention to the new members as individuals and offer help, in word and deed, to protect them against mistaking foolishness for cosmic wisdom.

It is inherent in the very nature of an esoteric society, however, that foolishness occurs every now and then. Thus, there have to be as many members as possible who can see through the foolishness and prevent it from being implemented. That includes what is in Mr. Goesch's letter.[8] He claims that promises have been made and not kept, and has tried to confirm this through a member who he believes or assumes has been promised something. When this member told him that this was not the case, Mr. Goesch, instead of admitting he was wrong, said that this was one more proof that magic is at work—when I shake hands with somebody on something, the handshake wipes out the promise in that person's memory. This is one of the main accusations in Goesch's letter.

It is obvious, my friends, that Mr. Goesch has not only written about these things, but has talked to a number of individuals about them. A vital interest in the affairs of the Society would really have required these people to go in all due haste to a more experienced member and make him or her aware of this situation. It is absolutely incomprehensible how anyone can allow Goesch to say something as impossible as, "When people tell me no promise has been made to them, the conclusion I come to is not that they really were not promised anything, but that their memory of the promise has been wiped out by the power of suggestion," and let it stand uncontested. When things like this are allowed to happen unhindered, then clearly the Society is not viable and cannot be used as a vehicle for esoteric truths.

There are two things, my friends, that are very much on my mind. One is the fact that everything I know compels me to consider bringing spiritual science to human beings as both necessary and urgent. But I am equally aware of another fact, namely, that the instrument established for this purpose is in the midst of a crisis. That is why I cannot help "tormenting" you with what I had to say yesterday and today. After all, meetings to take remedial action have been announced. But if these meetings run their course the way they did in earlier, similar cases, we will get nowhere.

Please be aware that the simple measure of expelling someone will never accomplish anything. Expulsion cannot resolve any concern of the Society. As you recall, we expelled Dr. Hugo Vollrath many years ago, and he managed to do everything he did later on in spite of having been expelled.[9] The same thing will happen in similar cases. It is possible to expel a member, but that is not enough; we cannot rest content with that.

If you will get out *Theosophy*, which is the first book I wrote in the theosophical movement on the subject of theosophy, and read the chapter entitled "The Path of Knowledge," you will find certain things that, if you think them through, will make it easy for you to come up on your own with what I said yesterday and today.[10] It is all there in that chapter. However, I must assume that not even this very first book of mine has been understood, for if it had been, many recent events could not have taken place.

When the special members' meeting takes place tomorrow, we must be sure that we are looking at these things with all due seriousness and dignity.[11] We need to ask ourselves whether we really want to let things get to the point where we have to admit that spiritual science cannot be disseminated by means of a society like this one. If that is the case, if it becomes impossible to do this through the Society, then we will need to find other ways of dealing with what is left behind as its corpse, and that will be much more difficult.[12]

I am not responsible for making the agenda for tomorrow, but how that agenda is dealt with will play a part in deciding whether the Anthroposophical Society will continue to exist in the future. Therefore, I will content myself with making an urgent appeal to you to deal with this situation with the greatest possible responsibility and to not gloss over things that are of the utmost significance for human civilization as a whole.

Tomorrow there will be a eurythmy performance at half past ten, followed by a lecture.

Swedenborg:

An Example of Difficulties

in Entering Spiritual Worlds

DORNACH, SEPTEMBER 12, 1915

MY FRIENDS, today I would like to talk about difficulties encountered in attempting to enter the spiritual worlds, and I will begin with a specific example. All of you will have heard of the seer Swedenborg.[1] I have often talked about him and have always emphasized that a personality like Swedenborg is not to be dismissed lightly. On the other hand, for those who really want to know what it takes to gain access to the spiritual worlds, visionaries like Swedenborg can serve as an example of how people can still be subject to all kinds of illusions in spite of having entered the spiritual world. The spiritual world is open to them, but that does not mean they are able to break free from the world of illusion.

I said that Swedenborg is not to be taken lightly. He was not one of those seers who lightheartedly give in to their visionary gifts without knowing much about life or about the world. Swedenborg was a profound thinker and an important scholar, certainly one of the greatest of his time, if not the very greatest. His scholarly knowledge encompassed everything the science of his day had to offer. A whole committee of experts has recently been formed to prepare for publication, not what Swedenborg left behind as a seer, but his purely scientific writings—substantial proof indeed of his well-founded scientific approach and striving for the truth.[2]

Swedenborg, then, in his pre-clairvoyant days, before being granted access to the spiritual world, had already accomplished so much that a whole committee of scholars is now needed to edit the great number of manuscripts documenting the sum total of his knowledge. (And in fact, these manuscripts may represent only a portion of what he knew.) This task is beyond the scope of any single expert of today. And we are talking only about his writings that have nothing to do with seership. Swedenborg was already at the peak of a career in academic science when he became clairvoyant—only then did the spiritual worlds become accessible to him. Swedenborg, then, was not simply some ordinary man who one fine day decided to call himself a visionary. On the contrary, he ascended to the level of seership on the basis of an eminently serious and conscientious scientific approach.

However, when we look closely at Swedenborg's clairvoyance, we can see how it is possible for a seer to stop short at a stage that does not yet lead on to the ultimate in knowledge.

This outstanding scholarly and clairvoyant personality clearly illustrates how necessary it is to be extremely conscientious when we talk about entering the spiritual worlds and about what can be brought back from them. I cannot emphasize strongly enough that before his clairvoyance developed, Swedenborg was already an outstanding scholar who had not only absorbed all the knowledge his age had to offer, but also added to it through many scientific discoveries of his own. This fact is already well established, and will undoubtedly become even more apparent once his unpublished works appear in print. He had made some first-class scientific discoveries before becoming a seer.

Swedenborg reported a great variety of information gained through clairvoyant perception.[3] It is interesting to note that when his soul ascended to the heights and he could look into the spiritual worlds, he always felt he was surrounded not only by his own aura, but also by numerous spiritual beings embedded in it. This is very characteristic and quite significant. Whenever Swedenborg's gift of clairvoyance became active, he immediately experienced that he was not alone—he felt his soul expand to embrace his aura and saw in it spiritual elemental beings proceeding from his own organs, as it were. As Swedenborg watched, these beings held counsel among themselves and also with Swedenborg himself, with his own soul.

From the very beginning, then, he was advised by these spiritual beings that are present in each human being. These inner beings were joined by others Swedenborg was able to recognize on the basis of their consultation with the beings that proceeded from within himself. He recognized some of these beings coming toward him as beings of the outer elemental world, and others as beings who have their home on other planets of our solar system.

It so happened that once, after having consulted with his own elemental beings, he recognized certain beings in his surroundings who demonstrated a certain peculiarity. So far, Swedenborg's clairvoyant perception had always allowed him to understand to a certain extent the language of both the elemental beings coming from within himself and the beings coming from Venus, Mercury, the Sun, and so on. He was accustomed to thinking that spirits have an understandable common language—the language of ideas, of the inner weaving of ideas come alive. I have told you about these ideas come alive in several recent lectures.[4]

Swedenborg was accustomed to understanding this language, which is also our basis for cultivating the art of eurythmy. When someone uses sounds in order to speak, the whole complex of forces that exists in order for speech to be able to resound is concentrated in the larynx and adjacent organs. Thus the human being as a totality is freed from having to "act out" speech. This means that the inner structure of speech becomes unconscious, subconscious—it becomes something totally earthly. Eurythmy is meant to enable us once again to participate with our whole being in speech.

But more on the deeper meaning of eurythmy some other time, my friends. For now I only want to point out that Swedenborg had always been able to understand the language of spiritual beings, until a certain moment when he noticed spirits approaching him who, like the others, spoke to him through all kinds of gestures and movements of their limbs or of their actual form, which is how all spirits speak. As I said, Swedenborg was used to understanding the spirits' gesture-language. This time, however, he could see the spirits making certain movements, but was unable to understand them; their movements conveyed no sense or meaning to his soul. He was surprised by that, as surprised as we would be if we were approached by somebody whose lips were moving in speech, but we could hear nothing.

Swedenborg learned a very significant lesson from this after realizing that these beings he could not understand were inhabitants of Mars—that there were in fact beings from Mars whose speech could not be understood even by someone who usually understood the language of spiritual beings. I am talking here only about Swedenborg's experiences. Because he made a point of studying these things rather than simply interpreting them arbitrarily, he gradually realized why he could not understand these souls from Mars. It was because they belonged to a group of cosmic beings who had developed the ability to conceal all their feelings and intentions, to not let anything of what they were feeling flow into their words. The fact that they were able to conceal their emotions and keep them to themselves made Swedenborg realize that hearing words and seeing gestures is not all there is to understanding language—something of the speaker's emotional state flows over to us as well. Understanding speech is actually based on this flow of emotional content. He realized that because these Mars beings had developed the ability to conceal their feelings, the meaning of their speech was not revealed in spite of the fact that they actually were speaking.

A short time later Swedenborg had another experience that led to an additional insight. He came to the realization that the beings from the hierarchy of the Angeloi did understand these Mars beings. He could not understand them, nor could the spirits proceeding from his own body, but the beings belonging to the class of the Angeloi could understand them. This realization was a very deep and meaningful experience for him. Not being able to understand something that was quite clearly understandable to the hierarchy of the Angeloi made him aware of the limits of his own visionary potential for perceiving the spiritual world.

We must avoid simply glossing over an account like Swedenborg's, because it can actually lead us deep into certain mysteries of the spiritual worlds. In order to understand the connection, let us recall several things I have described before. I explained how authentic seership begins, how good seers have to acquire a totally different relationship to the spiritual world than they have to the physical world. I told you that we perceive external beings and objects out there on the physical plane as existing outside us. We face these objects and take something of them into ourselves in the process of perception. Our I knows about the objects and creates mental images of them. This is the experiential basis of any kind of knowing and perceiving on the physical plane—we make mental images of the objects on the physical plane and recognize them.

I have also told you that this basic experience changes as soon as we ascend to spiritual worlds. There it is replaced with a different fundamental experience, the experience of oneself as object. Our I relates to the beings of higher worlds in the same way that objects formerly related to the I. We no longer perceive, but experience that we are being perceived, that the spiritual beings of the higher hierarchies are observing us. This experience of being perceived and observed by the Angeloi, Archangeloi, and other spiritual beings is a total reversal of our former relationship to the physical world. We achieve the awareness that our being has expanded to encompass the sphere of the hierarchies, and that the hierarchies are at work in us and are looking at us just as we used to look at objects on the physical plane.

Without this fundamental experience our whole relationship to the spiritual world is wrong, just as our whole relationship to the physical world would be wrong if we lacked the basic experience of perception and developing mental images. "I am observing" is true of the physical world; ultimately, "I am being observed" is true of the spiritual world.

However, right at the threshold into the spiritual world, we come to a region or current where we still retain the whole structure and essential characteristics of our relationship to the physical world. There, we have not yet rid ourselves of the attitude of "I am observing" and are not yet able to proceed to "I am being observed." Out of deeply embedded habits, we expect the spiritual world to be essentially a copy of the physical world—a subtler or more refined copy, but a copy nonetheless. And so there are more than a few people who imagine that being at a gathering of spirits would be just like standing here in this room among physical human beings—the spirits would be assembled just like people on the physical plane, but they would be a bit less dense, so you could stick your hand right through them. Because we bring our habits of perception from the physical plane into the spiritual world and retain our underlying mode of experiencing things, we are left with the illusion of being able to "observe the cosmic beings," and cannot ascend to that other fundamental experience of being observed by them.

44

As a seer, Swedenborg never freed himself from this illusion, at least not during the incarnation we're talking about. He was never able to ascend to the experience of being observed. If you read everything Swedenborg wrote as a visionary, you will find that he really does describe the higher worlds as if they were nothing more than a misty emanation of the physical world—figures that are very fine and vapor-like but otherwise very similar to those in the physical world.

It's true that Swedenborg describes the world of Imagination very aptly, but he is in no position to assess it because he veils the whole spiritual world in his habits derived from the physical world. That is why all the beings of the spiritual world only reveal to him what they are able and willing to clothe in the form of Imaginations derived from the physical world. In other words, Swedenborg sees only as much of the spiritual world as can be clothed in Imaginations contaminated with habits retained from experience on the physical plane. He sees mighty and important spiritual beings, no doubt, but always in a guise that is not their own, a guise that he himself imposes on them. And when he enters a region where the spirits make every effort to conceal what is within them—like the Mars beings who have learned to conceal their inner life and not reveal it in how they speak—he can no longer understand them; they remain a mystery to him. This lies at the root of all of Swedenborg's very conscientious descriptions, and to understand what Swedenborg's visionary world was like, we need to be aware of it.

Thus, if we really want to enter the spiritual world, we must try to identify our own self with the things around us in such a way that we become accustomed to breaking free of ourselves as we look at higher worlds. I have described this in the last chapter of *Theosophy*; basically, all the indications are already given there.[5] If we become accustomed to doing this, we will gradually begin to experience things in the other way I described. This is not something we can accomplish purely through our own efforts; all we can do is set out on the right path. The experience of being perceived by spiritual beings of the higher hierarchies comes to us as an act of grace on the part of the spiritual world itself. And it is not simply that higher beings look at us; we become perceptions, concepts, and thoughts for the beings of higher worlds in the same way that objects on the physical plane are for us.

If Swedenborg had been able to get used to being perceived and thought about by the beings of the higher hierarchies, then he would not have experienced the inability to understand the Mars beings while the Angeloi could understand them. He was only capable of applying his own perspective and could not make use of the angelic mode of perception. But that is precisely what we have to be able to do. It is not enough to have concepts; we must become concepts. It is not enough to think; we must become thoughts, thoughts of the beings of the higher hierarchies.

We must learn to stand in the same relationship to the beings of the higher hierarchies as our own thoughts stand in relationship to us. Swedenborg could not do that. If he had been able to do it, he would have known that as long as he remained within himself he would not be able to understand those Mars beings. However, if he had stepped outside of himself and become an object, a thought, an idea for the Angeloi, then, as expanded self, he would have been able to understand both the Angeloi and that category of Mars beings. He would then have had the same understanding of the essential nature of these Mars beings as the Angeloi had. He was unable to reach this stage because he always remained within the limits of his own consciousness and was never able to let the Angeloi observe and experience him, so that he himself would simply be their field of perception. If he had been able to do that, he would have known what the Angeloi know, for our knowledge of higher worlds comes through higher spirits, spirits of the higher hierarchies, knowing in us.

The important thing for us to keep in mind is that at this stage of evolution, the human constitution is such that we can know only about those worlds that are accessible to our organs of perception. If we want to transcend this limitation, we must open ourselves up to the consciousness of spiritual beings above us so that what these beings experience becomes the content of our own consciousness. It is important for us to experience ourselves as being included in the choirs of the spiritual beings. If you read everything I have written on the subject of initiation, you will find that all this has already been described there.[6]

The example of an important personality like Swedenborg shows us that it leads to illusions if we ascend to spiritual worlds without being steeped in the ability to step out of the kind of consciousness we apply on the physical plane. We are met by an illusory world. My friends, if you go through all the available visionary literature and read its descriptions of the spiritual world, what you will find for the most part will be illusions of this sort. It is important not to let yourself be deceived by these illusions, because being deceived by illusions at the threshold to the spiritual world is much worse than it would be to fall prey to illusions in the physical world.

We need to use our anthroposophical literature to gradually and rationally discover how we as human beings are meant to relate to the spiritual world. We are presented with a double opportunity to do so, first of all through the fact that this material is available, and secondly because of the fact that it cannot be read without considerable mental effort. I have always made sure of that, even though it has often been suggested that I make my writing more accessible to the general public. I have always resisted such suggestions because these things are just not meant to be popularized.

If we presented what we have to offer in our spiritual-scientific literature in all kinds of watered-down versions for the sake of popularizing it, we would simply be pandering to people's unwillingness to exert themselves, and asking for trouble at the same time. Attempts at loading up on spirituality in easy and thoughtless ways always lead to trouble. The effort we make in learning to understand something difficult to read is a kind of inner training and contributes to shaping our relationship to the spiritual world in the right way. It is an essential part of our literature, or at least it should be, that you really have to think in the most comprehensive way possible while taking in the information; your thinking has to become active. Everything you have at your disposal as a result of prior reading and experience must be brought into connection with the content of our anthroposophical writings.

At this juncture, I would like to demonstrate a particular train of thought as an example of how anthroposophical material can be studied actively and thoughtfully. I once gave a lecture cycle in Munich on the subject of the history of creation with reference to the Bible, in which the working of the Elohim was discussed.[7] This cycle is read frequently, and many people think that when they have read it and gotten it into their heads after their usual fashion, they have really accomplished something special. But that is not all there is to it. First of all, of course, it is important to accompany the reading of a cycle like this with a certain amount of inner effort. The train of thought could be as follows:

The Elohim, led by the being who later became the Christ, are a category of beings who had a particular task during the stage of planetary existence we call the Sun stage, when the main thrust of their development was taking place. Because of their particular connection to the Sun stage of existence, we must address the Christ, too, as a Sun being. We can give a lot of thought to how truly Sun-related the Elohim are. The whole tone of the lecture cycle shows that the Elohim's relationship to the Sun underlies the whole thing and can be felt throughout.

After thoroughgoing meditation—not in deep sleep!—we realize how we need to conceive of the character of the Elohim. Then, having immersed ourselves patiently in the character of the Elohim, we will experience after some time that a thought occurs to us, coming toward us from nowhere in particular. For example, it might occur to us—and this is just an example—that Jehovah, one of the Elohim, forbade eating from the Tree of Knowledge, and that after the Luciferic temptation, once human beings had in fact eaten from the Tree of Knowledge, they were barred from also eating from the Tree of Life. How strange that the Elohim should speak of trees!

I have often said that the language of a document such as the Bible should not be taken lightly. If trees are spoken of in the Bible, if the Elohim speak of trees, you can be sure it's significant. Something essential is meant by this expression. It has been said of Homer that he declared that each thing has two names, one in the language of the gods and one in the language of ordinary mortals. With this in mind, we might imagine that the gods' referring to trees may have something to do with this divine language. Considering the subject more deeply, we may wonder what the Elohim are actually talking about when they speak of the Tree of Knowledge and the Tree of Life. What do they mean?

If you consider our teachings in their entirety, my friends, you will realize that the Tree of Life and the Tree of Knowledge must have something to do with the essence of the human being. Being forbidden to eat from the Tree of Knowledge means, as you will eventually discover, that the human soul is not to strive for the kind of knowledge bound to the physical body. This has led to the kind of sense-bound perception we know today. "Eating from the Tree of Knowledge" means becoming bound up with the physical body to the extent that the kind of knowledge brought about by Lucifer now prevails, as I described in a recent lecture.[8] Thus, the Elohim were referring to something inherent in human beings when they spoke of the Tree of Knowledge. And they must also have meant something intrinsic to the human being when they spoke of the Tree of Life.

We may wonder why we see as we do today, how it came

about that we perceive as we do. It came about because our soul and spirit, permeated with the being of Lucifer, have become embedded in our physical body and are consuming it, although this is not what was originally intended. This physical body is the Tree of Knowledge, and the ether body is the Tree of Life. After having let themselves be seduced by Lucifer into using their physical body for purposes of perception as we know it now, human beings were prevented from also acquiring knowledge through the ether body. That has been denied us. If you are really thinking, my friends, you will arrive at trains of thought like this one.

The next question to be asked, then, is why the physical body is called the Tree of Knowledge in the language of the gods. Why do they call it a tree, and why do they also call the ether body the Tree of Life? Why are they talking about trees? It is easy to understand what is meant by this if you recall that the gods in question evolved during the Sun period for the most part and thus assumed some essentially Sun-like qualities. For a moment, just reflect on the fact that during the ancient Saturn period, everything was at the mineral level, while during the ancient Sun period, everything was at the evolutionary stage of plants. Since the gods we call the Elohim developed their characteristic way of speaking during the Sun period, it is natural for them not to speak of things that could only be experienced later, during the Moon and Earth stages of evolution, but about what evolved in the universe during the Sun stage, namely plant life. When using their own language, which is the language of the Sun, it is only natural for them to speak of trees.

You see, my friends, this is the kind of thing you can come to simply by taking what is in my books and lecture cycles and thinking it through in the right way. It is not enough to go on reading and reading and reading and putting together things you have read; you need to go further in your own thinking and use the means suggested by the very nature of things themselves to draw connections between them. But in doing that, you are also doing something else: You're making a real effort, and the result of this effort is that your soul becomes independent. However, this takes work, real work. I have to emphasize again and again that it is not through passively giving ourselves up to something, but through using our own soul forces to grapple with it actively, that we begin to separate the spiritual world from the physical world.

Active effort is what counts in attempts to gain access to the spiritual world. If you really want to enter the spiritual world, you cannot shy away from working through what confronts you and bringing it into connection with everything life has given you. Without this effort, all kinds of crazy things can happen—like someone believing he is the reincarnation of Homer but feeling no need to do anything to prove that something of Homer's genius is welling up in him. Since Homer already put in all the effort, the person in question can spend this incarnation comfortably lying on the couch in mystical slumber! If you make an effort to actively work through whatever confronts you, you will not be diverted into all kinds of mystical monkey business. Instead, you will eventually reach the point where you can develop an appropriate sense for the deeper meaning the spiritual world's truths hold for human beings. Then you will realize that you have to make every effort not to allow your habitual ways of thinking, feeling, and perceiving on the physical plane to get mixed up with qualities belonging solely to the spiritual world.

This attitude is crucial, my friends, and once we have really acquired it, it will prevent us from doing anything foolish in our efforts to enter the spiritual world. It doesn't require any particular effort to eat salt for a week in an attempt to descend to subearthly realms, and then eat no salt for a week in an attempt to ascend into higher elemental realms. That takes no effort at all, but there is also nothing to be gained from it except the worst kinds of illusions. Inner work is the only way to really accomplish something in the spiritual world. And inner work, if it is really taking place, will by its very nature lead you to the right thoughts and keep you from getting into trouble with regard to the spiritual world. Without it, however, we are subject to perversions of mystical thinking, and people have every right to laugh at us then.

For example, I once received a letter from a man of sound common sense who said that he had visited a member of an anthroposophical branch and found that people kept all the windows closed although it was terribly hot. I have nothing against closing windows, especially when everything said indoors can be heard outside—that would be a sensible reason for closing them, wouldn't it? But instead of telling him that, people said, "Dr. Steiner has expressly told us to close the windows when lectures are given in our branch, so that the demons can't get in." This man, who was quite unspoiled by mysticism, wrote to me asking why spirits couldn't get in through closed windows. What kind of an esoteric teacher is that, he wondered, who tells his pupils to close the windows so the demons do not get in? You can see how the physical plane is confused with higher worlds in this kind of careless talk. It is quite true that beings on the physical plane cannot get in through closed windows, unless they break them, but we will hardly be able to keep the spirits out by shutting the windows! We really must develop appropriate and serious concepts to apply to the spiritual and physical worlds.

If we give it some thought, the example of Swedenborg, who was conscientious and energetic and a splendid seer in his own way, can help us correct some fundamental errors in our own way of thinking. More on this subject tomorrow.

LECTURE FOUR

Methods and Rationale
of Freudian Psychoanalysis

DORNACH, SEPTEMBER 13, 1915

CONSIDERING the kind of deliberations you are engaged in at the moment, my friends, I must assume that your minds would be less than ready to take in a continuation of yesterday's lecture. For those of you who want to hear it, that lecture will be given tomorrow, but today I would like to speak about something that will relate in some way to things you all must necessarily have in mind at the moment.

First of all, and from a very specific point of view, I would like to address the question of what is really confronting us in the Goesch-Sprengel case. In recent lectures I have often said that it is important to arrive at the appropriate perspective from which to try to resolve any given issue. How, then, can we arrive at the right perspective on this particular matter through objective study of the case?

In order to deal with a case like this objectively, we must first of all remove it from its personal context and insert it into a larger one. If, as I believe, this larger context turns out to be what is most important for our anthroposophical movement, we will find ourselves obliged to study this case for our own edification and for the sake of spiritual science itself. And in fact there is a larger context to the case, as will become apparent if we look at Mr. Goesch's letter of August 19 with an eye for his main motives and arguments.

Since you have important deliberations ahead of you, I will not detain you too long, but will only select a few essential points for your consideration. The first is Goesch's claim that promises have not been kept. If you listened to the letter carefully, you will have noticed that the emphasis in his reproach is not on the alleged making and not keeping of promises. His primary accusation is that I looked for and systematically applied a means of making promises to members and not keeping them, and that once the members noticed that these promises were not being kept, they were put into a state of mind that forced them into a particular relationship to the one who had made and not kept the promises. As a result, forces accumulated in their souls that eventually made them lose their sound judgment.

So the first hypothesis Goesch presents is that systematic attempts were made to stifle the members' good sense, that deliberately making and breaking promises was a means of dulling their normal state of consciousness, resulting in a kind of stupefaction that turned them into zombies. That is the first point his letter addresses.

His second point has to do with one of the means of carrying this out. To put it briefly, through handshakes and friendly conversations and the like, I am supposed to have initiated a kind of contact with members that was suited, because of its very nature and the influence it allowed me to exert, to bringing about the above-mentioned effect on their souls.

A third thing we must keep in mind as a red thread running through Goesch's whole letter is the nature of his relationship to Miss Sprengel. We could add to these three points, but let us deal with them first.

To begin with, how does Goesch manage to construct such a systematic theory, based on his first two points, about how steps were taken to undermine the members' state of consciousness? We need to go into this thoroughly and try to find out where it comes from. In Goesch's case, we are led to his long involvement with Dr. Freud's so-called theory of psychoanalysis.[1] If you study this theory, you will begin to see that it is intimately related to how the pathological picture presented in the letter develops. Certain connections can be drawn between this pathological picture, as it relates to Goesch's first two points, and his involvement with the Freudian psychoanalytic point of view.

Of course, I am not in a position to give you a comprehensive picture of Freudian psychoanalytic theory in brief—my intent is only to present a few points that will help clarify the Goesch-Sprengel case. However, in a certain sense I do feel qualified to talk about psychoanalysis, because in my earlier years I was friends with one of the medical experts involved in its very beginnings.[2] This person eventually abandoned the theory of psychoanalysis after it degenerated later on in Freud's life. In any case, please do not take what I am going to say now as a comprehensive characterization of Freudian theory; I only want to highlight a few points.

Freudian psychoanalysts start from the assumption that an unconscious inner life exists alongside our conscious soul-activity—that is, in addition to the soul-activity we are conscious of, there is also an unconscious inner life we are usually not aware of. An important component of psychoanalysis is the doctrine that certain experiences people have in the course of their life can make impressions on them, but these impressions disappear from their conscious awareness and work on in their subconscious. According to the psychoanalysts, we do not necessarily become fully conscious of these experiences before they sink down into the unconscious—for example, something can make an impression on a person during childhood without ever coming to full consciousness, and still have such an effect on that person's psyche that it sinks down into the unconscious and goes on working there. Its effects are lasting, and in some cases lead to psychological disturbances later on. I am skipping a lot of links in the chain of reasoning and jumping right to the outcome of the whole process. In other words, we are to imagine in the soul's subconscious depths a kind of island of childhood and youthful experiences gone rampant. Through questioning during psychoanalysis, these subconscious proliferating islands in the soul can be lifted up into consciousness and incorporated into the structure of conscious awareness. In the process, the person in question can be cured of psychological defects in that particular area.

During the early years of the psychoanalytic movement, it was the practice of Dr. Breuer in particular to carry out this questioning with the patient under hypnosis.[3] Later on, this practice was discontinued, and now the Freudian school conducts this analysis with the patient in a normal waking state of consciousness. In any case, the underlying assumption is that there are unhealthy, proliferating islands present in the psyche below the level of consciousness.

This psychoanalytic outlook has gradually spread to incorporate and try to explain all kinds of phenomena of ordinary life, particularly with regard to how they appear in people's dreams. As I already explained once in a lecture to our friends in another city, it is at this point that the Freudian school really goes out on a limb in saying that unfulfilled desires play a primary role in dreams.[4] Freudians say that it is typical for people to experience unfulfilled desires in their dreams, desires that cannot be satisfied in real life. It can sometimes happen—and from the point of view of psychoanalytic theorists, it is significant when it does—that one of these desires present on an unconscious island in the psyche is lifted up in a dream and reveals in disguised form an impulse that had an effect on the person in question during his or her childhood.

Please note the peculiarity of this train of thought. It is assumed that as young boys or girls, people have experiences that sink down into subconsciousness and work on as fantasy experiences, clouding their consciousness. The pattern, then, is this: experiences of waking life are repressed and continue to work on the subconscious, leading to a weakened state of consciousness. This is exactly the same pattern Goesch constructs with regard to promises being given and broken and working on in the subconscious—all with the intention to create the same effect in the subconscious as the "islands" in Freudian psychoanalytic theory. According to Goesch, this was done cunningly and deliberately and resulted in a state of stupefaction analogous to what occurs when experiences of waking life have sunk into subconsciousness and are brought up again in a dream.

Psychoanalytic theory is a very tricky business, and if you dwell on it long enough, it gives rise to certain forms of thought that spread and affect all your thinking. As you can see, this has something to do with why Goesch came up with such a crazy idea.

In addition, as I have said before, the concept of physical contact plays an important part. I am now going to read certain passages from one of Dr. Freud's books, a collection of essays from the Freudian magazine *Imago*, and I ask you to pay close attention to them.[5] But I must precede that with something else concerning the Goesch-Sprengel case. Those of you who have known Miss Sprengel for some time will recall that she was always very concerned about protecting herself from other people's influence on her aura—she lived in horror of having to shake hands and things like that. Even before Goesch arrived on the scene, she had already gotten the idea that shaking hands is a criminal act in our esoteric circles. The following incident is absolutely typical: I had business to do in Dr. Schmiedel's laboratory and happened to meet Miss Sprengel there.[6] I extended my hand to her, which gave her grounds for saying, "That's how he always does it—he does whatever he wants to

you and then shakes hands, and then you forget all about it."
There you have the origin of that theory about handshaking.
Yesterday you all heard what this theory became in Miss
Sprengel's confused mind with the help of Goesch. He contrib-
uted his understanding of Freud's theories and combined things
systematically with Freudian ideas.

The following passage is from page 29 of the above-mentioned book by Freud:

> The principal characteristic of the psychological constellation
> which becomes fixed in this way is what might be described
> as the subject's ambivalent attitude (to borrow the apt term
> coined by Bleuler) towards a single object, or rather towards
> one act in connection with that object. He is constantly wish-
> ing to perform this act (the touching), [and looks on it as his
> supreme enjoyment, but he must not perform it] and detests
> it as well. The conflict between these two currents cannot be
> promptly settled because—there is no other way of putting
> it—they are localized in the subject's mind in such a manner
> that they cannot come up against each other. The prohibition
> is noisily conscious, while the persistent desire to touch is
> unconscious and the subject knows nothing of it. If it were
> not for this psychological factor, an ambivalence like this
> could neither last so long nor lead to such consequences.[7]

This is followed by a long discussion of the role fear of physical contact plays in cases of neurosis:

> In our clinical history of a case we have insisted that the
> imposition of the prohibition in very early childhood is the
> determining point; a similar importance attaches in the subse-
> quent developments to the mechanism of repression at the
> same early age. As a result of the repression which has been
> enforced and which involves a loss of memory—an amnesia—
> the motives for the prohibition (which is conscious) remain

unknown; and all attempts at disposing of it by intellectual processes must fail, since they cannot find any base of attack. The prohibition owes its strength and its obsessive character precisely to its unconscious opponent, the concealed and undiminished desire—that is to say, to an internal necessity inaccessible to conscious inspection. The ease with which the prohibition can be transferred and extended reflects a process which falls in with the unconscious desire and is greatly facilitated by the psychological conditions that prevail in the unconscious. The instinctual desire is constantly shifting in order to escape from the impasse and endeavours to find substitutes—substitute objects and substitute acts—in place of the prohibited ones. In consequence of this, the prohibition itself shifts about as well, and extends to any new aims which the forbidden impulse may adopt. Any fresh advance made by the repressed libido is answered by a fresh sharpening of the prohibition. The mutual inhibition of the two conflicting forces produces a need for discharge, for reducing the prevailing tension; and to this may be attributed the reason for the performance of obsessive acts. In the case of a neurosis these are clearly compromise actions: from one point of view they are evidences of remorse, efforts at expiation, and so on, while on the other hand they are at the same time substitutive acts to compensate the instinct for what has been prohibited. It is a law of neurotic illness that these obsessive acts fall more and more under the sway of the instinct and approach nearer and nearer to the activity which was originally prohibited.[8]

Considering the obsessions involved in fear of physical contact, you can well imagine how it would have been if Miss Sprengel, as a person suffering from this fear, had ever been seen by a psychoanalyst who, in line with usual psychoanalytic practice, would have questioned her about her fear of contact and tried to discover what caused it.

A third factor I want to emphasize is the relationship of Miss

Sprengel to Mr. Goesch. According to psychoanalytic theory, this relationship would of course be characterized by the presence of repressed erotic thoughts. I mean that quite objectively....[9]

At this point, my friends, we must look a bit more closely at the whole system of psychoanalysis. As I have just outlined for you, psychoanalysis lifts up into consciousness certain "islands" in the unconscious psyche, and it assumes that the majority of these islands are sexual in nature. The psychoanalyst's task, then, is to reach down to the level of these early experiences that have sunk into subconsciousness and lift them up again for purposes of healing. According to Freudian theory, healing is brought about by lifting hidden sexual complexes up from the depths of the subconscious and making the person aware of them again. Whether this method is very successful is a matter of much discussion in books on the subject.

As you can see, psychoanalysts' thinking is often colored by an underlying pervasive sexuality, and this is taken to extremes when psychoanalysis is applied to any and all possible phenomena of human life. For example, Freud and his disciples go so far as to interpret myths and legends psychoanalytically, tracing them to repressed sexuality. Consider, for example, how they interpret the story of Oedipus.[10] In brief, the content of this legend is that Oedipus is led to kill his father and marry his mother. When psychoanalysts ask what this story is based on, they conclude that such things always rest on unconscious, repressed sexual complexes usually involving sexual experiences in earliest childhood. The Freudians are firmly convinced that a child's relationship to his or her father and mother is a sexual one right from birth, so if the child is a boy, he must be unconsciously in love with his mother and thus unconsciously or subconsciously jealous of his father.

At this point, my friends, we might be tempted to say that these psychoanalysts, if they actually believe in their own theory, should apply it to themselves first and foremost, and admit that their own destiny and outlook stem from an excess of re-pressed sexual processes experienced in childhood. Freud and his disciples should apply this theory to themselves first. They derive the Oedipus legend, for instance, from their assumption that most little boys have an illicit emotional relationship to their mother right from birth, and are thus jealous of their father. Thus, the boys' father becomes their enemy and works on as such in their troubled imagination. Later, however, they realize rationally that this relationship to their mother is not permis-sible, and so it is repressed and becomes subconscious. The boys then live out their lives without becoming aware of their forbidden relationship to their mother and their adversarial rela-tionship to their father, whom they experience as a rival.

According to psychoanalytic theory, then, what we need to do in cases of defective psyches is to look for psychological complexes, and we will find that if these are lifted up into con-sciousness, a cure can be effected. It's too bad that I can't pre-sent these things in greater detail, but I will try to give you as exact an outline of them as possible. On page 16 of the above-mentioned book, for instance, you can read the following:

> There has been little opportunity in the preceding pages for showing how new light can be thrown upon the facts of social psychology by the adoption of a psycho-analytic method of approach: for the horror of incest displayed by savages has long been recognized as such and stands in need of no further interpretation.[11]

This essay explains why primitive peoples so strictly enforce the ban on marrying one's mother or sister and why relation-ships of this type are punished. "Incest" is love for a blood-relative, and one of the first essays in this book is entitled "The Horror of Incest." This fear is explained by assuming the exis-tence of a tendency to incest on the part of each male individual in the form of a forbidden relationship to his mother.

All that I have been able to add to our understanding of it is to emphasize the fact that it is essentially an infantile feature [that is, primitive people retain this for a lifetime, while in civilized children it is repressed into the subconscious] and that it reveals a striking agreement with the mental life of neurotic patients. Psycho-analysis has taught us that a boy's earliest choice of objects for his love is incestuous and that those objects are forbidden ones—his mother and his sister. We have learnt, too, the manner in which, as he grows up, he liberates himself from this incestuous attraction. A neurotic, on the other hand, invariably exhibits some degree of psychical infantilism. He has either failed to get free from the psycho-sexual conditions that prevailed in his childhood or he has returned to them—two possibilities which may be summed up as developmental inhibition and regression. Thus incestuous fixations of libido continue to play (or begin once more to play) the principal part in his unconscious mental life. We have arrived at the point of regarding a child's relation to his parents, dominated as it is by incestuous longings, as the nuclear complex of neurosis.

Thus, according to psychoanalytic theory, the central complex involved in neurosis is a boy's forbidden sexual attraction for his mother and sister.

This revelation of the importance of incest in neurosis is naturally received with universal skepticism by adults and normal people. Similar expressions of disbelief, for instance, inevitably greet the writings of Otto Rank, which have brought more and more evidence to show the extent to which the interest of creative writers centres round the theme of incest and how the same theme, in countless variations and distortions, provides the subject-matter of poetry. We are driven to believe that this rejection is principally a product of the distaste which human beings feel for their early incestuous wishes,

62

now overtaken by repression. It is therefore of no small importance that we are able to show that these same incestuous wishes, which are later destined to become unconscious, are still regarded by savage peoples as immediate perils against which the most severe measures of defence must be enforced.[12]

From this point of departure, an atmosphere of sexuality spreads until it pervades the psychoanalysts' whole field of activity. Their whole life is spent working with ideas about sexuality. That is why psychoanalysis has been the biggest contributing factor in making an unbelievable mockery of something quite natural in human life. This has crept into our life gradually, without people noticing it. I can sympathize deeply with an old gentleman by the name of Moritz Benedikt (who spent his life trying to bring morality into medicine) when he says that if you look around, you'll find that the physicians of thirty years ago knew less about certain sexual abnormalities than eighteen-year-old girls in boarding school do today.[13] This is the truth, and you can really empathize with this man. I mention it in particular because it is really extremely important to regard certain processes in children's lives as simply natural, without having to see them in terms of sexuality right away.

Nowadays, these complicated psychoanalytic theories lead us to label a lot of what children do as sexually deviant, although most of it is totally innocent. In most cases, it would be enough to regard these things as nothing more than childish mischievousness that could be quite adequately treated with a couple of smacks on a certain part of the anatomy. The worst possible way of dealing with it, however, is to talk a lot about these things, especially with the children themselves, and to put all kinds of theoretical ideas in their heads. It is hard enough to talk about these things with grownups with any degree of clarity. Unfortunately for people who are often called upon to provide counseling, parents frequently come with all kinds of complaints, including some really dumb ones, about how their children suffer from sexual deviance. Their only basis for these complaints is that the children scratch themselves. Now, there is no more sexuality involved in scratching yourself anywhere else than there is in scratching your arm. Dr. Freud, however, upholds the idea that any scratching or touching, or even a baby's sucking a pacifier, is a sexual activity. He spreads a mantle of sexuality over all aspects of human life.

It would be good for us to look more closely at Freudian psychoanalysis in order to become aware of the excesses of materialistic science; specifically, of those of psychoanalysis in seeing everything in terms of sexuality. In a book introduced by Dr. Freud, the Hungarian psychoanalyst Ferenczi writes about the case of a five-year-old boy named Arpad.[14] There is no doubt in his mind as to the sources of Arpad's interest in the goings-on in the chicken run:

> The continual sexual activity between the cock and hens, the laying of eggs and the hatching out of the young brood gratified his sexual curiosity, the real object of which was human family life. He showed that he had formed his own choice of sexual objects on the model of life in the hen-run, for he said one day to the neighbour's wife: "I'll marry you and your sister and my three cousins and the cook; no, not the cook, I'll marry my mother instead."[15]

We could wish for a return of the days when it was possible to hear children say things like this without immediately having to resort to such awkward sexual explanations. I can only touch on this subject today, but I will discuss it at greater length sometime in the near future in order to reassure all you fathers and mothers.[16] But of course, Freud's theory, which is spreading widely without people noticing it, is only a symptom of a worldwide tendency. And when parents come with the complaint that their four- or five-year-old sons or daughters are suffering from sexual deviance, in most cases the appropriate response is, "The only deviant thing in this case is your way of thinking about it!" In most instances, that is really what's wrong.

My intention in telling you all this has been to point out the kind of atmosphere Freudian psychoanalysis is swimming in. I am well aware that the Freudians would take issue with this brief characterization. But we are fully justified in saying that psychoanalysis as a whole is positively dripping with this psychosexual stuff, as its professional literature reveals.

Suppose the assumption that psychosexual islands exist in the human subconscious actually proves to be true in the case of a certain individual. A Freudian theorist might subject that person to questioning and be able to add a new case history to the annals of Freudian psychoanalytic theory. In the case concerning us, Goesch might have undertaken this line of questioning and made some discoveries among those psychosexual islands that would have served to verify Freud's theories. But to do that, Goesch would have needed to be stronger in his own soul. As it was, however, he succumbed to a certain type of relationship to his new lady friend. The material in our possession supplies ample evidence of this relationship and will allow anyone who applies it in the right way to describe their relationship with clinical, objective precision.

Since what can be learned from a specific case is often of greater significance than the actual case itself, let me point out that this case can lead us to the same conclusions I presented in my essay, published in the *Vienna Clinical Review* in 1900, entitled "The Philosophy of Friedrich Nietzsche as a Psychopathological Problem."[17] Notwithstanding all the contributions Nietzsche's genius made to the world, it was necessary to point out that Nietzsche would be misunderstood if the psychopathological factor in him were not taken into account. It is important for our Society that psychopathological elements not gain the upper hand, that they be eradicated from our minds and seen in the right light so that psychopaths are not looked upon as some kind of higher beings. That is why it is also important to see the current case in the right light and assess what is actually involved from the right standpoint.

It is already too late for me to describe now at length how the storm developed. When I was in Vienna in May of this year, one of our members wrote me a letter I had to tear up on returning here, since taking letters across the border is no longer allowed. This letter contained accusations very similar to those raised by Goesch under the influence of Miss Sprengel and showing a similar involvement in Freudian psychoanalysis. They came from the same quarter; the same wind was blowing in both sets of accusations. In fact, if I could have read you some sentences from that letter, they would have sounded remarkably like what Miss Sprengel inspired in Goesch.

What, then, was actually going on in the Goesch-Sprengel case? Goesch could not really function as a psychoanalyst, because to do that his relationship to Miss Sprengel would have had to be an objective one like that of a doctor to a patient. Her influence on him was too overwhelming, however, and thus his involvement in the examination was not fully conscious and objective. In Freudian terms, everything at work in the psyche of his friend, the "keeper of the seal," came out, but since it sank down into Goesch's unconscious, it was masked by the whole theory that came to light in his letter.

The Goesch-Sprengel case grew out of one of the greatest mistakes and worst materialistic theories of our time, and we can only deal with it by realizing that both people involved threw a mantle of secrecy over their human, all-too-human relationships. In essence, this consisted of shrouding their relationship in Freudian psychoanalytic theories, as the documents very clearly reveal.

When we attempt to help people who come to us in such a confused psychological state, they are often fawning, enthusiastic supporters to begin with, but later on their adulation changes into enmity. That, too, can be explained in psychoanalytic terms. However, our most urgent concern at the moment is our relationship to the rest of the world. Just as we are now experiencing hostility coming from the direction of psychoanalysis, steeped as it is in sexuality, we can expect to encounter at any moment new opposition from all kinds of aberrations resulting from other all-too-human impulses.

This shows us that we must study such cases; they should be of great interest to us precisely because our Society represents a spiritual movement. I could speak at much greater length on this subject, but I must stop for today because you need to get on with your deliberations. I simply wanted to point out the first tentative steps we must take in seeing where the dangers for our movement lie and how urgent it is that we all do as much as we can to help the world out there learn that we are not chicken-livered. We know how to stand up for ourselves. When things come up in disguise as they did in this letter, we must rip off the mask and expose where they come from. Their origins lie much deeper than we usually think; they originate in the materialistic outlook of our times, which has not only become the dominant view in science but has contaminated our life as a whole. Combating it is our movement's very reason for existence, but we must keep our eyes wide open and see what is going on in the world. We must recognize what the people coming to us have learned out in the world and what they bring with them when they come to us.

LECTURE FIVE

Sexuality and Modern Clairvoyance: Freudian Psychoanalysis and Swedenborg as a Seer

DORNACH, SEPTEMBER 14, 1915

YESTERDAY I inserted a talk on psychoanalysis into this lecture series, since that subject is of concern to all of us at the moment because of the case at hand. You will have noticed that I first characterized the psychoanalytic view as distinguishing between consciousness and the unconscious in our inner life. I then went on to describe, if only briefly, how the psychoanalytic point of view as a whole is swimming in sexuality, and you could see that with this second aspect, an extremely unfortunate (you might even say "terrible") element has entered our culture. This points to something characteristic of current intellectual trends in general.

There can be no doubt that in distinguishing an unconscious that exists alongside the conscious mind, psychoanalysis has made a legitimate contribution to our culture. We can look at it like this: These people are on the right track in thinking that the human soul goes beyond what our ordinary consciousness encompasses. However, these same people have also taken their materialism to extremes. It has done more than engulf their thinking, which is what happened in the case of what is now erroneously known as monism. The materialism of the psychoanalysts, however, also pulls the lower human drives into their theory and incorporates them into it. As a result, sexual drives, the most subjective element possible, become the motivating impulse in scientific activity.

We must look particularly closely at such modern cultural phenomena, because they show us that something independent of human individuals is compelling even the crassest materialists among us to recognize a higher spiritual element than the one we are immediately aware of. After all, the followers of Freud are deeply rooted in materialism, in their intellect as well as their instincts; yet the objective world compels even them to investigate something beyond the scope of ordinary consciousness. That is the objective side of the matter.

On the other hand, the subjective aspect is that these people are so tangled up in materialism that their lowest and most subjective drives are immediately drawn into the business of formulating their outlook on life. That is part and parcel of materialism just as much as the left hand belongs to the right hand or the left eye to the right eye. And tumbling right down into the very lowest human drives is the inevitable consequence of getting stuck in materialism if people really let themselves go.

However, my friends, we can really understand this way of looking at the world only if we can get to the bottom of many a riddle of the world order. The dangerous thing about philosophies like psychoanalysis is that people are on the right track, but drag their impure instincts into what is true. It is much less harmful when impure instincts are incorporated into something completely erroneous than it is when they are incorporated into a partial truth. And the truth in the psychoanalytic view lies in its recognition of the fact that so much of what is at work in human life is unconscious, truly unconscious. That is where psychoanalysts are on the right track and have come upon many things that are true and correct.

Let us follow up how psychoanalysts stumble onto the right track. In the book I told you about yesterday, the head of the psychoanalytic school of thought attempts to explain certain customs among primitive people on the basis of certain psychoanalytic theories. He does so in accordance with connections he assumes to exist between early childhood and neurotic conditions later in life.

We saw yesterday how the element of sexuality plays into these theories. In his book *Totem and Taboo*, in the essay "Taboo and Emotional Ambivalence," Freud compares some of the views and ideas of primitive people with certain infantile characteristics of civilized human beings that manifest in neuroses, in certain types of nervous or psychological disorders.[1] From what we discussed yesterday, you will recall that psychoanalysts explain many things as the result of impulses that affect people in the early years of their life and then retreat to islands in these people's psyche where they work on in the unconscious. This means that infantile psychological activity is still going on in civilized adults. According to this view, neurotics, or at least a certain type of neurotics, are walking around at age forty with psyches in which earliest childhood experiences, infantile experiences, are still especially influential.

Freud then compares certain primitive beliefs with the experience of neurosis. For example, he says:

A Maori chief would not blow on a fire with his mouth; for his sacred breath would communicate its sanctity to the fire, which would pass it on to the pot on the fire, which would pass it on to the meat in the pot, which would pass it on to the man who ate the meat, which was in the pot, which stood on the fire, which was breathed on by the chief; so that the eater, infected by the chief's breath conveyed through these intermediaries, would surely die.[2]

Freud does not compare this fear of blowing on a flame because of what might happen to someone eating out of the pot warmed by it with the habits of the person we have been speaking about for the past few days—after all, he did not know her and her fear of others affecting her aura. However, he does compare it to the behavior of someone else who came to him as a patient. He says:

> My patient's husband purchased a household article of some kind and brought it home with him. She insisted that it should be removed or it would make the room she lived in "impossible".[3]

That is what the patient tells the psychoanalyst. A spiritual scientist using healthy understanding to contemplate a patient like this would have to consider the problem from many different angles. Psychoanalysts, too, might or might not be able to follow the clues in a case like this. And a false mystic might come up with all kinds of profound ideas about magical influences at work on this person or proceeding from this very refined personality who has reached such an advanced stage of evolution that she cannot tolerate having certain objects in the same room with her!

The psychoanalyst says of his patient:

> She had heard that the article had been bought in a shop situated in, let us say, "Smith" Street.

He finds out that she has heard that the item in question was bought in a store on Smith Street—increasing mystification! He continues:

> "Smith," however, was the married name of a woman friend of hers who lived in a distant town and whom she had known in her youth under her maiden name. This friend of hers was at the moment "impossible" or taboo.

That is, it was something she did not want to come into contact with.

Consequently the article that had been purchased here in Vienna was as taboo as the friend herself with whom she must not come into contact.

As the psychoanalyst in question has found out, the patient had had a friend with whom she had once gotten into trouble. The friend's name was Smith. This fact survives on an island in her psyche. Nothing of it is present in her ordinary waking consciousness, but although she is unaware of the connection, it remains in her unconscious. Only the name provides the connecting link inasmuch as the friend whom she hated in her youth—a hatred the patient was not conscious of—is called Smith and the article in question was bought on Smith Street. The similarity of the names provides the connection; that is how the subconscious works up into the realm of consciousness.

People with a strong mystical bent make much of names that sound alike. They make such associations very readily and are led to all kinds of mystical conclusions without ever becoming fully aware of the connection. For example, it could happen that a person who once played the role of Persephone might come to believe that she was an actual reincarnation of Persephone because she thinks she once heard someone she didn't know call out the name Persephone as she went past. It could well be, however, that she simply overheard someone saying he saw a woman telephoning, and that she understood "Persephone" from that sequence of sounds. The person in question misheard "Persephone" when what was actually said was "telephoning," and that is enough for her to go on spinning her mystical threads. This is all strictly hypothetical, of course, but it does correspond to how such things can actually happen.

I could give you many other examples from the essays of Dr.

Freud and his followers that would show you that the philosophy of psychoanalysis is in fact seeking the relationship between the conscious and the unconscious. However, as I described yesterday, as a result of certain tendencies of our times, all it finds down there in the unconscious is sexuality. This is an extremely important point, and we must take a very close look at it.

The day before yesterday, I told you about Swedenborg and his clairvoyance, for in his own way, Swedenborg was an extremely distinguished and advanced clairvoyant. I explained that he was characteristically unable to cross the threshold into a different state of consciousness, to say "I am being observed" instead of "I am observing." Swedenborg always wanted to observe everything himself. He observed his Imaginations. He himself was not being observed from the sphere of the Angeloi, but was observing that sphere with the same kind of consciousness he used on the physical plane. Let's take a good look at this once more so as to be clear about the right way to ascend from the physical plane to a higher plane of existence. We must be very clear that on the physical plane, we perceive various objects which are mirrored by means of our physical body and thus become our concepts. That's how we arrive at the important insight that we are looking at objects, and this is the basis of our consciousness.

As soon as we ascend to a higher state of consciousness, however, all this changes fundamentally. There we are received with our I by beings of a higher order, and then we become aware of being perceived, of being looked at by them.

Swedenborg presents a third state of consciousness in which a whole world of objects not present on the physical plane is perceived by him exactly as he perceived objects on the physical plane, although in a more refined state. Thus Swedenborg perceives spiritual objects presented to him in the form of Imaginations just as if the spiritual world were nothing more than a finer version of the physical world. He looks at the spiritual world in the same way we look at the physical world in everyday life. What is the cause of this?

We have already traced the process Swedenborg went through. He discovered certain spiritual beings who made it clear to him that they came from Mars. These beings were incomprehensible to him because they repressed all expressions of emotion and expressed themselves only in thought-gestures. As I told you on Sunday, he realized that he could not understand these beings because they had acquired the ability to conceal their soul life. If Swedenborg had been able to see with the kind of consciousness available to the Angeloi (which is what would have happened if he had really ascended to the spiritual world—that is, if he had also carried his consciousness up into the spiritual world), he would have been able to understand the nature of these Mars beings even though they concealed all their emotions. As it was, however, the content of the Mars beings' soul appeared to Swedenborg as a cold world of thoughts. This is all very strange.

Just think how terribly afraid most people here on the physical plane are of the cold and abstract world of reason. You hear all kinds of derogatory comments about this cold and abstract world of thoughts, and people do everything possible to try to avoid it, to avoid thinking in pure thoughts. Someone who expects people to ascend to pure thought is held to be out of touch with and hostile to real life. That's how people on the physical plane feel about the abstract world of thoughts.

This point of view is very widespread. I will give you an example; present company is always excepted, of course, so I am sure there will be no hurt feelings. For a number years now, a great many people have been reading my *Philosophy of Freedom*, which is a work of pure thought.[4] It first appeared in the 1890s. It would be interesting to find out how many of the people in our movement who are now reading *The Philosophy of Freedom* would have read it on its own merits, without knowing anything about me and our movement, if it had fallen into their hands back in the early 1890s. How many people would have read it back then and how many would have said, "I can't get through this tangled web of thoughts; it just doesn't make any sense!"? You can just imagine, then, how many people are reading this work of pure thought for strictly personal reasons. (Present company excepted, of course.) The only ones who are reading it for other than personal reasons are the ones who would have read it even if they had never met me in person. We have to admit to this quite soberly; it shows how horrified we on the physical plane are of so-called abstraction.

In spite of being such a great scholar, when Swedenborg encountered the beings I described, this particular class of Mars beings, on the astral plane, he was incapable of understanding the pure thoughts, free of any emotion, that were active in their souls. Transferred to the physical plane, this is the same as if someone would say about *The Philosophy of Freedom*, "It's all Greek to me; no sensible person can read that kind of language," meaning that it seems totally incomprehensible. In the same way, Swedenborg found these Mars beings incomprehensible on the astral plane.

It is important, however, that we at least have the good will and make the effort to advance to the kind of thinking that is free of emotion—to begin with, free of the emotions we know so well in ordinary life. If the content of *The Philosophy of Freedom* appeals to people because their feelings incline them to a more spiritual way of looking at things, they have not yet achieved pure thinking. Only those people who take it in because of the thoughts' logical sequence and the way they support each other are relating to the book in the right way.

Swedenborg, on the other hand, in spite of being such a great scholar, could not conceive of being drawn to a world of pure thoughts free of emotional motives. We must try to understand, my friends—and the means of doing so are available in our anthroposophical literature—to what extent in everyday life our choice of truths is dictated by emotional impulses, by impulses provided for us on the physical plane through our karma or upbringing. We are only free of subjectivity when we have really moved on to a realm of thinking in which thoughts sustain each other and no longer have any subjective content.

After that, however, there is still one more thing we must accomplish. When we have really reached the stage of thinking in pure thoughts, when a sequence of pure thoughts is present in our soul, then our personal mind or subjective I is no longer involved. This accounts for the severity we experience when we reach this stage of pure thinking. It is no longer possible to bend things to fit into the mold of how we subjectively would like to have them. Take a train of thought like that of *The Philosophy of Freedom*. It is impossible to construct it in any other way. It cannot be arbitrarily tampered with; you have to let it grow inside you like a living organism. Then your I is really uninvolved; it is thinking itself that is doing the thinking.

However, your thinking only becomes mature if what it has been emptied of—your own I—is replaced with something else. In place of the contents of your personal mind, the mind-content of spirits belonging to higher hierarchies must fill this emotion-free thinking. When you have come so far as to be able to gradually rid your emotion-filled thinking of its subjective content so that it contains only pure concepts, then divine content, the content that comes from above, can flow in.

Swedenborg never reached this stage. In spite of being a great scholar, he could not extricate what he was thinking from his personal emotions. When he ascended to the astral plane, beings such as the Mars dwellers who could think in pure thought were completely alien to his thinking, confined as it still was to his own personality, and they were therefore incomprehensible to him. As far as he was concerned, their gestures could not be understood at all. But why was Swedenborg barred from entering the world of higher consciousness? Why did he carry a mode of perception appropriate to the physical plane up into the spiritual world, to which he really did gain access? We need not investigate why certain spirits were able to keep their thoughts free of subjective emotional content, but why was Swedenborg unable to understand their words and gestures?

The answers to all these questions will become apparent if we first ask what was actually going on in Swedenborg's case and what he took with him onto the astral plane. It seems he was not completely able to extricate his spiritual nature from his physical person, for if he had been able to do so, he would have seen his I as an object in the realm of higher consciousness. His I would have become like a remembered object, something like the broken pots in a comparison I used some time ago. He was unable to wrest himself sufficiently free of himself. However, as you know from what I have already said about him, it was characteristic of Swedenborg's clairvoyance that he did not just see illusions. He did not just see maya—he could actually recognize objective facts; for instance, he knew he was dealing with beings from Mars and could see what they were like. That was all correct, but he was seeing the spiritual world in its maya-aspect, through a veil of illusion, so to speak. He was in fact looking at real beings from Mars, but could not understand that they were actual *spiritual* beings.

Now, my friends, let me ask you to be really, really clever for a moment, and clever in a way that people who want to develop their clairvoyance usually are not. Obviously, Swedenborg did not perceive these beings from Mars with his ordinary senses, with his ordinary sense of sight. After all, he was seeing them in the spiritual world. In other words, he could not see them with his sense of sight or hear them with his sense of hearing or even understand them with his ordinary capacity for thought. As I have explained to you, this capacity for thought was actually a gift of the ancient Moon stage, that is, something that developed before the Mars forces came into play....[5] [*gap in the stenographic record*]. Among all the powers of cognition known to human beings, there was nothing that could have enabled him to understand these beings.

Thus we are confronted with the strange fact that Swedenborg undoubtedly recognized the beings he saw, but did not recognize them by means of any higher forces. He recognized them by means of some ability he should not have had because he was lacking the necessary consciousness—ordinary powers of consciousness on the physical plane are inadequate to explain what he was seeing. But in that case, how was he actually seeing? Now, Swedenborg had spent his life not only as a great scholar but also as a very pure person, and so a certain energy was transformed within him. All people on the physical plane have this energy, which is somewhat similar to clairvoyant ability. On the physical plane, however, it is used for a different purpose. What was this energy that enabled Swedenborg to see as he did?

Swedenborg was seeing by means of a force that perceives outer appearances without touching them in any way and without making use of the eyes. What kind of a force is that? On earth, on the physical plane, it is the force that comes to expression in sexual activity, the mysterious force that pulls people together in earthly love, a force different from all other powers of perception. Swedenborg had stored up this force, and when he reached a certain age it was transformed in him, although it remained sexual energy in some respects. He used this sexual energy to see spiritual worlds. That is, transformed sexual energy is actually the basis of Swedenborg's clairvoyance.

You can conclude from all this that human beings during their evolution on earth are provided with a force that expresses itself as sexuality during earthly life, but that will be transformed once it is no longer bound to the physical body. On the other hand, you can also come to the conclusion that the forces leading to clairvoyant vision are very intimately related to forces involved in what are now the lowest drives in human nature, and that one of these realms can be attracted by the other, so to speak.

My friends, it follows that clairvoyance is not something to be toyed with. Of course, what I have just said does not apply to spiritual science as such, but it does apply to all kinds of clairvoyance people grab for in passing without working to acquire it legitimately. We cannot take seriously enough the fact that clairvoyance is not to be developed by simply applying a transformation of our usual mode of perception on the physical plane to higher planes of existence. These higher planes require that we work toward a new mode of perception applicable to the spiritual world, a mode of perception that has nothing to do with sexual energy, since that is physical and exists only for the physical plane. Applying the same mode of perception to higher worlds as is applied on the physical plane, that is, the assumption that people can still perceive in the same way as they do on the physical plane, is what makes people relate clairvoyance and sexual energies.

There are several ways of avoiding this, and we are now at a crucial point in human evolution where these things must be understood. What I have just told you is ancient knowledge, and in olden times people knew how to protect themselves. They knew that people approaching the spiritual world had to recognize both their own weakness and the fact that strength of character, inner discipline, and doing away with any unrestrained emotional impulses are necessary for ascending into the spiritual worlds in the right way. Ancient initiates were aware of human weakness and took steps to prevent any possibility of mixing the two spheres.

How did they do it? Simply by keeping people away from the opposite sex whenever truly spiritual matters were being spoken of. That is, the female sex was not allowed to participate in gatherings in which spiritual scientific matters were discussed. That is why in the past women were excluded from all spiritual-scientific gatherings. This measure prevented the men from mixing the two spheres in any way, because they were bound by strictest oath not to discuss what went on in the lodge outside the lodge itself. Women, then, could have no connection to spiritual science other than the white gloves, which were a significant symbol of this whole state of affairs.[6]

Now these times are long gone, and spiritual scientific movements such as ours should attempt to do away with such constraints. However, the spiritual realm must still be kept totally free of the other sphere I mentioned; these two realms are not to be mixed.

What we have seen recently is a case of the worst possible mingling of spheres, a case in which sexual drives were at work but were interpreted as something quite different. They were interpreted as all kinds of mystical things, but in reality they were sexual drives. It is important to face this fact squarely and to understand it from the inside, out of the inner nature of the cosmic order. Only our recognition of the very great dignity and solemnity of spiritual life can guard us against egotism in spiritual activity. Once egotistical mysticism enters, nothing can save us from mixing the two above-mentioned spheres in the worst possible way.

Thus we saw how in Swedenborg's case, repressed sexuality filled his Imaginations that would otherwise have remained empty, but only to a certain extent. When he came into contact with beings who were able to eliminate all emotions from their gestures, he was no longer able to fill that sphere, which was a strictly human one and came about because his sexuality extended to include his Imaginations. Swedenborg, then, is a good example of what to avoid in approaching the spiritual world in modern times. Aspirations that resemble Swedenborg's in any way put people striving for clairvoyance in danger of arousing the sphere of sexuality and having the two spheres mingle.

My friends, we must be able to speak of these things as a matter of course in spiritual scientific contexts. It would be very unfortunate if we were unable to mention them objectively and scientifically, because serious seekers also need to know the dangers they face in their search. That is also why it is so easy for an impure fantasy to misinterpret pure spiritual striving.

We stand at an extremely significant point in our spiritual scientific communications, and what I wanted to do today was sketch the lines converging in this point. Because I want to be very thorough in speaking to you about these things, I will continue to present my reflections on this question tomorrow. We will meet again at the same time, or at whatever time seems best—we can decide that before we leave here today.

LECTURE SIX

The Concept of Love
As It Relates to Mysticism

DORNACH, SEPTEMBER 15, 1915

LET US continue with the theme we have been considering for the past few days and begin by asking the question, "How old is love?" There is no doubt in my mind that the great majority of people with their rather superficial way of looking at things would immediately respond that love is as old as the human race, of course. However, anyone who recognizes cultural history as being imbued with spiritual impulses, and who therefore tries to deal with such issues concretely instead of in vague generalities, would answer quite differently. Love, my friends, is seven hundred years old at the most!

Nowhere in ancient Greek and Roman prose or poetry will you find anything resembling our modern idea of love. And if you read Plutarch, for instance, you will find the two concepts of Venus and Amor very clearly differentiated.[1] Love as the subject of so much lyrical eloquence in literature, and especially in poetry, is no more than six or seven hundred years old. Our modern notion of love—what love means to us today and how that is instilled in people—has played a part in the human heart and mind only for the past six or seven centuries. Before that, people did not have the same idea of love; they did not speak about it in any even remotely similar way.

This should not come as a surprise to you, not even on a theoretical or epistemological level. The objection that human beings have always made a practice of loving does not hold good; that would be like saying that if the Earth revolves around the Sun as the Copernican view claims, then it must have been doing so even during Roman, Greek, and Egyptian times—in fact, as long as it has been in existence. Of course that's true, but the people of those times didn't talk about the Copernican system.

Similarly, it is also not valid to object that what is expressed in the idea of love must have existed before the concept itself was there. Of course, the facts and phenomena of loving have always been an identifiable facet of human life, but people have not always talked about them. We have come a long way in the past six or seven hundred years in that respect; in fact, we have come so far that love occupies a central position in many people's view of life. And not only that, we now have a scientific theory, the theory of psychoanalysis, which is positively swimming in the most vulgar concepts of love, as I have shown. This is an evolutionary tendency that anthroposophists in particular are called upon to resist and to transform by fostering a spiritual-scientific philosophy of life.

Many of you may be aware that I described these same things quite precisely from a historical perspective in some earlier lectures, so I would be surprised if you were all taken aback by my statement that our idea of love is only six or seven hundred years old.[2] In any case, the idea of love has gradually crept into all kinds of philosophical concepts during the past few hundred years, as is revoltingly evident in psychoanalysis. It would take a long time to get to the bottom of all this, but I hope these more or less aphoristic remarks will give you some clues.

As an example, let's consider a contemporary thinker who is

totally immersed in modern cultural concepts—in other words, someone who cannot overcome his supposed insight that outer sensory-physical reality is all we can reasonably talk about. I have already introduced Fritz Mauthner to you as a very sincere representative of this type of person.[3] Mauthner is a linguistic critic and the author of a philosophical dictionary. This puts him in a very strange position in that it makes him aware of the fact that the word "mysticism" has existed down through the ages—as a linguistic critic, he naturally wants to know what stands behind both the word itself and actual mystical aspirations.

My friends, just consider how much reading material we have to struggle through to understand that particular relationship of the human soul to superearthly worlds that deserves the name "mysticism." Consider, too, how very seriously we have to take any explanations, such as those in *Knowledge of the Higher Worlds*, if we want to understand the inner attitude needed in order to face the spiritual world as a mystic—that is, as a soul at one with the spiritual pulse and flow of higher worlds.[4] We can only really say what mysticism is in the modern sense of the word when we have engaged in serious reflection such as that in *Knowledge of the Higher Worlds*. In other words, we have to at least study that book thoroughly and attentively a couple of times.

When someone like Fritz Mauthner gets his hands on a book like *Knowledge of the Higher Worlds and Its Attainment*, it is patent nonsense to him—just so many words. Mauthner is an honest man, after all. He would be telling the truth if, having read Swedenborg, he were to say that he doesn't understand a thing when Swedenborg talks about inhabitants of Mars who can conceal their innermost impulses. He might also say that he finds nothing to relate to in a book like *Knowledge of the Higher Worlds*; perhaps angels might be able to understand it, but he cannot.

This is an utterly plausible opinion, and I am convinced it is what Fritz Mauthner would come to as an honest person. And in fact, if he is honest and sticks to the truth, coming to this conclusion is inevitable because the concept of mysticism eludes him entirely; there's nothing to it as far as he is concerned. For him, everything in *Theosophy* or *Knowledge of the Higher Worlds* is all just words, words, words.[5] If he himself experiences a kind of Faustian striving, he might express it by saying, "[I will] contemplate all seminal forces in the outer physical world and be done with peddling empty words."[6] And in his own way, he is quite right.

However, Mauthner is not only honest, he is also thorough, and so he wonders if it is actually true that human souls have never experienced anything like mysticism. After all, people have always talked about it. What was it, then, that induced them to speak about mysticism?

When I was a very young man, I knew an outstanding theologian, now dead, who was also very well educated in philosophy.[7] He always said, and rightly so, that behind every error there is something true and real we must look for. No idea is so crazy that we need not look for the reality behind it. This is also Mauthner's rationale in conceding that there must be something to mysticism after all. Obviously, there are still strange characters around who write books like *Knowledge of the Higher Worlds* and talk about our mystical relationship to spiritual worlds, but to him it is all nonsense. However, there has to be something in human nature that produces the emotions these crazy, mixed-up people call mysticism. There must be something behind it.

If you try to find how Mauthner discovers what underlies mysticism, the most you can say after having read the entry on mysticism in his dictionary is that he keeps going around in circles.[8] Everything in this article revolves around words and definitions of words. But since I was interested in finding out how Mauthner, in his own way, attempts to get at what is behind mysticism, I looked it up in his dictionary to see what could be found there...[*gap in the stenographic record*]

So I looked up not only his entry on mysticism but also the

one on love. I found the article on love to be one of his best, and very well written. It's actually very nice. Mauthner first mentions Spinoza's definition of love and Schopenhauer's brief and heavy-handed definition, and then he explains that it is necessary to distinguish between mere eroticism, which is strictly physical and confined to sexuality, and real love on a soul level. Mauthner admits all that, and even goes on to say something as elevated as this:[9]

I believe that people who are one-sided geniuses in thinking have seldom, if ever, had any understanding of love in its highest degree, of feelings of love taken to pathological extremes. They have not experienced it personally and have only tried to categorize the descriptions of poets.

That is, the philosophers did not know much about love except what they looked up in books of poetry.

I believe that love in its ultimate degree has been experienced and described only by artists (approximately since the time of Petrarch), and that it entered common parlance through the power of imitation or fashion and captured the imagination of readers for six hundred years, and is now in the process of being replaced by another fashion. Although the ultimate degree of love is as rare as a great artistic creation or the kind of religious union with God that St. Francis may have experienced, still the whole world babbles on about religion, art, and love. What they mean by all this are mere substitutes for emotions that perhaps one person in a million has actually experienced.

So there!

The ultimate degree of love, whose existence I do not deny, is really something of a miracle—and people have also tried to explain miracles as pathological phenomena. In the most unlikely event that both sexual partners experience the highest degree of love, a miracle takes place in defiance of all the laws of nature: each one lifts the other and both float above the earth. Archimedes' principle is, or appears to be, superseded. Whether in happiness or in death, the longing of mysticism is fulfilled.

There you have it. For someone like Mauthner, steeped in modern materialistic philosophy, the emotion of love is the only way human beings can experience the feelings "deranged" mystics experience in their relationship to spiritual things. "Whether in happiness or in death, the longing of mysticism is fulfilled" is a remarkably honest sentence coming from someone who has lost all connection to the spiritual world. Mauthner continues:

For the purposes of this little investigation, I have deliberately overlooked many other meanings of the word "love." At this juncture, however, I must still point out that union with God is experienced by mysticism as the pleasure of love at its most passionate and most spiritual, and that Spinoza made use of his first definition of love (in Book III and Book V of his *Ethics*) to proclaim the love for God, the *amor erga Deum*, as the highest bliss known to human beings. The longing to give expression to the inexpressible is intrinsic to mysticism, and this has led to considerable misuse of the concept of love. There is something of this vivid mysticism not only in Spinoza's pantheistic extravagance, but also in Schopenhauer's metaphysical cynicism. It is also what Cousin meant when he said that we love the infinite and imagine we love finite things.

The well-known feeling that leads us to call our sexual partners "lovers" runs through so-called love in all its various degrees. And we describe our very subjective experience through the unwarranted use of the corresponding verb "to love." The attempt to find an objective noun, namely, the word "love" to describe this experience met with such success that people have persuaded themselves that the experience itself is as common as the word "love" has become.

As you can see, when the modern materialistic world tries to formulate a concept of mysticism out of its own fundamental impulses, it is forced to conclude that what mystics dream of can only be found in the emotion of love in the real world; that is, everything spiritual is dragged down into a refined version of eroticism.

It is typical, for instance, that Mauthner brings up the particular way in which a woman friend of Nietzsche's, the author Lou Andreas-Salomé,[10] describes Nietzsche's intellect as a type of refined eroticism.[11] It is interesting, too, how Mauthner reacts to her portrayal of Nietzsche. He says:

> Recently, after so many attempts by men, a woman, Friedrich Nietzsche's friend Lou Andreas-Salomé, has also tried to formulate a philosophy of love in her excellent book on Nietzsche, which won her the hatred of the entire Nietzsche clan. She is very subtle in her expositions, but bold enough to refuse to accept fidelity as an attribute of love, and she forges a link between the artist's fantasy and that of lovers ("Eroticism," p. 25). She too, however, intellectualizes the act to such an extent that there seems to be no conceptual distinction between sensuality and the intellectual phenomena accompanying it.

In other words, then, from the way men and women express themselves, we see that nowadays, even in our thinking, we have to replace our relationship to the spiritual world with the eroticism throbbing in our souls—a more or less refined eroticism, depending on the character of the individual in question.

This all has to do with the fundamental materialistic tendency of our times, which also leads to untruthfulness when people are not honest enough to admit that all they know about mysticism is the aspect that is identical to eroticism. Untruthfulness emerges when these people talk about eroticism but conceal it behind a veil of mystical concepts. Materialists who freely admit that they see nothing but eroticism in all of mysticism are actually much more honest than people who take eroticism as their starting point but hide it behind mystical formulas as they clamber up to the very highest worlds. Sometimes you can almost see the ladders they are using to scramble up to the very highest planes of existence in order to have a mystical cover-up for something that is actually nothing more than eroticism. On the one hand, then, we have the theoretical linking of mysticism to eroticism, and on the other hand the tendency of our modern times to sink down into eroticism and drag all kinds of murky, misunderstood mysticism into it.

Some time ago I challenged you to work on eradicating the mystical eccentricities that come about through the kind of mingling of spheres I described, so that people who are well able to recognize the noble character of spirituality will once again be able to rise to the perspective needed to speak about spirituality where spirituality is actually present, without clothing subjective emotions in spiritual forms. In making this appeal, I hoped to create some degree of clarity in these matters within the Anthroposophical Society, so that clear thinking might prevail.[12] Time alone will tell whether we will actually be able to accomplish this.

In former times (and in fact until quite recently, as I pointed out yesterday), a much more radical means was used to safeguard the basic requirements of any kind of spiritual scientific society. It was a simple matter of excluding one entire sex, half of humanity, so that the other half would be spared the dangers inherent in mixing elevated spiritual concepts with thoughts of natural human activity on the physical plane. Thinking about spiritual matters belongs to the spiritual world. We must come to the healthy realization that it is much worse to talk about certain aspects of natural human interaction in mystical formulas that do not belong to this natural level than it is to call these things honestly by name and admit that this aspect belongs to the physical plane and must remain there.

Schopenhauer, in his singularly heavy-handed fashion, characterized love as follows: "The sum total of the current generation's love affairs are thus the human race's 'earnest *meditatio compositionis generationis futurae, e qua iterum pendent innumerae generationes*'"—the earnest meditation of the human race as a whole on the composition of generations to come, on which in turn countless generations depend.[13] Well, that's Schopenhauer's opinion, not mine! It is a terrible thing to see people deny the rightful place of such urges and disguise them by saying, for example, that they are obliged to do what they do so that an extremely important individuality can incarnate. That is really an abomination in the eyes of someone trying to practice mysticism in all earnestness and dignity.

We must also take into account the fact that mysticism is not intended as an excuse for laziness on our part. That is what it becomes, however, when healthy concepts are replaced by unhealthy ones in the name of mysticism. Here on the physical plane, people are supposed to make their mark through good will and work—real hard work. If they prefer to gain recognition under false pretenses rather than on the merits of their work, and demand special treatment by virtue of being the reincarnation of somebody or other, then they are using mysticism as an excuse. They want to be recognized as someone special without doing a thing. This is a very trivial and vulgarized way of looking at the matter.

If we are making every effort, as indeed we must nowadays, to foster spiritual science openly in the presence of both sexes, the old compulsory bans must be replaced by a serious and dignified attitude on the part of both men and women as they seek to acquire knowledge of the higher worlds. We must succeed in eliminating from this search all the fantasies bound up with our lower human drives. Only then will we be able to prevent the proliferation of errors originating in the illusions of individuals prone to mystical laziness. Mysticism, my friends, does not ask us to become lazier than the people out there who care nothing about it. If anything, it requires us to be more diligent than they are. And mystical morality cannot mean sinking below the moral level of other human beings; rather we must advance beyond it. If we do not make a serious effort to eradicate anything resembling "Sprengelism," as I would like to call it, from our Society, we will make no progress.

How I will continue with this series of lectures depends on the course of your meeting today.[14] Let us first see how far you get in this meeting, and then I will announce when we will continue.

LECTURE SEVEN

The Philosophy of Psychoanalysis as Illuminated by an Anthroposophical Understanding of the Human Being

DORNACH, SEPTEMBER 16, 1915

TODAY I am simply going to add to what we talked about yesterday, and if possible, I would like to take up a new topic tomorrow.

In the fourth lecture in this series, I stressed that finding the right perspective is essential to understanding any subject, whether it is the world in general, an individual human being, social interactions, or any series of interrelated facts. The belief that the truth can be arrived at by proceeding to draw logical conclusions from some arbitrary point of departure is the source of a great many errors. If we really want to understand something, the first thing we have to do is to work out the right point of view from which to approach it. We must realize that finding the right perspective is essential to any studying we do; attempting to understand a subject by approaching it from an arbitrary starting point actually causes a lot of mistakes.

In the past few days we have been looking at the theory of psychoanalysis, a singularly revolting philosophy of life. In this instance, we can use this term freely without being in the least subjective. As we said, it is not its point of departure that makes psychoanalysis revolting—in fact, its starting point could equally well lead to correct conclusions if applied properly. It becomes revolting because of the way the people involved with it intrude their personal feelings and emotions. The fact that it has incorporated personal and subjective aspects is the reason why psychoanalytic theory is positively dripping with sexuality, as I put it before.

However, if people who are aware of the principle of first discovering the right perspective became acquainted with the psychoanalytic theory's point of departure and proceeded from there, the results would be quite different. They might incorporate certain materialistic affectations into psychoanalytic theory to begin with, but they would soon be forced to adopt purer and nobler means of understanding simply through having made the distinction between the conscious and the unconscious mind. They would realize that dragging in points of view of the sort we mentioned before is not objective but a sign of arbitrary emotions belonging to subjective human nature.

The most significant aspect of any true study is that it tends to lead us far beyond our original point of departure. Rather than incorporating our own subjective impulses into the subject, we are guided and spurred on by the subject itself. Eventually, every true student becomes aware of how truly necessary this principle is. It is indispensable in making any spiritual scientific world view into a reality and equally indispensable to the structure of a society in which such a world view is to be fostered. We must finally realize that we have to take anthroposophy seriously and give it the respect it deserves. That is, we must not incorporate previous subjective habits into things belonging to our spiritual scientific philosophy, but must rather let ourselves be guided by what that philosophy requires. For example, in everyday life someone may be in the habit of always arriving late instead of at the specified time. In ordinary bourgeois life, that habit may be merely unpleasant or less than advantageous for that person's advancement, but in our anthroposophical movement, the whole way we deal with spiritual scientific truths ought to make that kind of behavior an inner impossibility except in cases of dire necessity.

In the past few days, we have talked a lot about dignity—not only the essential dignity of spiritual science itself, but also the dignity of our own interactions within the Society. We saw how important it is for us to spend time together as members among ourselves, with no one else present. Of course, making sure we arrive on time is a superficial thing, but in the past few days people have still been coming late, even though the lectures started at twenty past six. If we carry on like that, my friends, we will never even be able to begin to realize the ideal of our Society. In the somewhat attenuated circumstances that come about when we cannot be sure that members will not continue to arrive once we have begun, we will never be able to rule out the possibility of having uninvited guests in our midst. It is simply inconsiderate to come late to a Society function when the Society needs to make sure that everyone present is actually a member; that is, when some of us have to go to the extra effort of keeping an eye on the people entering until all members are present. When the people standing at the door have come in, we need to be able to shut the doors and know that everyone is here.

It should certainly not be necessary to make a special point of talking about things like this, but in spiritual science we have to be guided by the concept of symptomatology, which simply means that any being tends to act the same way in important instances as it does in less significant ones. People who don't even manage to arrive on time for meetings will also not be able to act out of the requisite sense of responsibility when it comes to something important. A great deal of the damage that has

94

become so blatantly evident lately has come about because people were not particular enough about certain things. It is really important for us to conduct the practical affairs of anthroposophy with the conscientious exactitude I just mentioned. We have seen an example of how we as members of a spiritual scientific society interact on an ordinary everyday basis; this example, although very mundane, is nonetheless indicative of what spiritual science requires of us.

In our efforts to find the right perspective on what we have spoken about aphoristically so many times in the past few days, the main thing we have to keep in mind is that the structure and organization of the world as a whole consists of expressions and revelations of real spiritual entities. They are present behind the revealed world, which conceals them from our perception. As you know from many previous lectures, these beings are constantly in movement, constantly inwardly active. At the moment, I am not talking about any particular movement, but about their inner activity as a whole. We have to imagine a certain degree of complexity in this movement if we want to understand how the beings that stand behind certain phenomena relate to the phenomena themselves. The following example will be familiar to you from previous anthroposophical lectures.

We know that our physical evolution began during the ancient Saturn period and that it continued during the Sun period, when etheric development set in, and so on. But what does our physical development on ancient Saturn mean in relation to the structure of the cosmos as a whole? It would be totally inaccurate to take our physical nature as it is now and assume that if we imagine it in a much more primitive and simplified form, that's what the physical human being would have looked like during the Saturn stage. Nothing could be further from the truth. Perhaps it will help you understand this if I tell you that there is absolutely nothing in the present-day physical world, nothing on the physical plane as it exists now, that bears the slightest resemblance to human physical existence during the Saturn stage of evolution. In none of the forms and facts of the physical world as we know it now is there any trace of what human physical development was like during that evolutionary period. So if we want to understand this ancient form of our physical existence, we must make the effort to do so with a soul and spirit freed from the physical and etheric bodies.

I will call the world in which we understand the makeup of our earliest potential for physical existence during the Saturn stage [*writes on the chalkboard*] the world of the perception of physical human nature on Saturn. For the time being, let me just say that we must leave the physical body and undergo a higher form of development in order to achieve an understanding of structures corresponding to physical human nature during the Saturn stage.

Next, let us consider human physical existence during the Sun period, which represents a progression of physical evolution from the Saturn stage. It is impossible to understand our physical Sun nature with our present-day physical organs of perception. Once again, we must ascend into the spiritual world, but not as high as the level required for comprehending human physical nature during the Saturn period. In other words, we are able to investigate our physical Sun nature at a somewhat lower level. We can call this [*writes on the board*] the world of the perception of physical human nature on the Sun.

For investigating physical human nature as it evolved during the Moon period, a still less elevated level of perception is required. As soon as we become capable of body-free perception, we are able to comprehend everything that corresponds to our physical Moon nature. Let us call this third stage in the relationship of the human being to objective fact [*writes on the board*] the world of the perception of physical human nature on the Moon.

Continuing in the same vein, we come to our physical nature during the Earth stage of evolution. In order to understand this, we do not even need to leave the physical body; we can grasp it with our physical organs of perception. This level of cognition is the natural one for human beings during life on Earth, and we can call it [*writes on the board*] the world of the perception of physical human nature on Earth.

So, my friends, we have looked at four different levels of the worlds of perception, levels that can also be called [*writes on the board*] physical plane, soul world or astral plane, spirit world or Devachan plane, and higher spirit world or higher Devachan plane.

Higher spirit world, higher Devachan plane		World of perception of physical human nature on Saturn
Spirit world Devachan plane		World of perception of physical human nature on Sun
Soul world astral plane		World of perception of physical human nature on Moon
Physical plane		World of perception of physical human nature on Earth

If you follow what I have been describing, you will know that we have to place the physical human being of the Saturn stage here, the physical Sun-human here, the Moon-human here, and the earthly physical human being here [*small circles*]. This in no way contradicts our usual concepts, but is indicated quite clearly in my book *An Outline of Occult Science*, where I described at length how what we recognize as human physical nature at the Moon stage is not to be observed on the physical plane, but at a higher level, and so forth.[1] It's all explained there very clearly.

Today we know that human beings have descended during the course of their physical evolution [*line connecting the small circles*]. The human being, to the extent that we are speaking of our present-day physical nature, is a descending spiritual being. This is one of the basic ancient principles of any spiritual science. Thus, when considering our physical body, we must realize that everything we can see of it at this Earth stage in evolution is that aspect of ourselves that has descended the furthest.

However, there is also something concealed in the physical body. It conceals something that is actually Moon-like in nature, something more hidden that is Sun-like in nature, and something still more deeply hidden that is Saturn-like in nature. Thus, within the revealed physical body, inner character and inner essentiality are concealed. In a sense, we can actually perceive only a quarter of our physical body. The other three quarters are concealed behind the perceptible body and are nobler and more spiritual in nature than the aspect visible on the physical plane.

Looking at any part of our physical body as it exists now on the physical plane, we have to realize that all our physical organs are in constant inner movement; they are constantly descending and evolving from the spiritual toward the physical. We must understand that as they are growing and developing into their proper form on the physical plane, all our organs are involved in a descending course of evolution. They are in the process of evolving downward from a more spiritual form of existence to a more material one.

In assessing the nature and character of anything belonging to a human being, we must be guided by the rule of always finding the right point of view. We are led to the right perspective when we realize that from a certain point of view—the one I have been discussing today—physical human nature is in a process of descent. Therefore, when we look at human development from childhood to maturity, the childhood stage of evolution must be regarded as more spiritual and the mature stage as more material, since a descent from the spiritual to the material has taken place in between. We will not understand human physical development if we look at it from any other point of view. It is only possible to understand it if we are aware that a descent of the physical human being takes place during growth and development, that a growing human being allows something spiritual to descend deeper into matter.

The same principle applies to the world as a whole. Thus, we also speak of cultural evolution. For instance, once upon a time there was an ancient Indian cultural epoch that evolved into the ancient Persian epoch, then into the Egypto-Chaldean-Babylonian epoch, then into the Greco-Latin epoch, and finally into our own cultural epoch. However, we also know that former cultural epochs continue to exist alongside more recent ones. I have showed you how this manifests in language.

Applied to the human being, this can show us how physical organs that have proceeded further along the course of descent can exist side-by-side with others that are still at earlier stages. We will gradually come to see that according to this principle, we can distinguish two systems of organs within the human being, although for today, I will only point this out aphoristically.

Let us first consider our senses and all the organs that allow us to have sensory perceptions. In terms of their physical structure, these sense organs are all at a certain level; the spiritual has streamed downward to a certain level in these organs. I'll make you a diagram of that [sketches on the board]. Now, we said that human nature in its entirety consists of a downward flow; it is moving in this direction [arrow]. The upper horizontal mark indicates the position of the senses within this downward flow, so we must think of all the organs of sensory perception as being at level A.

Next, let's look at a different system of organs, for instance the respiratory system. In order to consider this, too, from the right point of view, we must find the level to which it has descended. Eventually, we will find that the respiratory system stopped at level B. While our sensory system descended to level A, our respiratory system continued to descend until it reached level B.

As you might imagine, this process of descent can go on still further, so there could even be a system of organs that has descended still further, to level C. And in fact, our sexual organs have done just that.

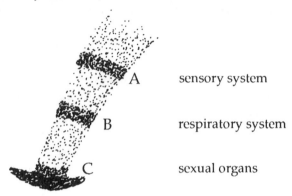

A   sensory system

B   respiratory system

C   sexual organs

Eventually, our physical evolution reached its lowest point and a gradual re-ascent began. However, we will not be able to talk about that today. I will indicate the lowest point of descent with this curved shape at the bottom of the diagram. This is where the earthly process of descent stopped. You can tell from all this that our sensory organs are much more spiritualized than our respiratory organs and everything else. And, as we will come to understand ever more clearly, our sexual organs represent the lowest level of descent. Therefore, all other components of our physical human nature are more spiritual than that particular system of organs.

That was easy enough to understand, wasn't it? However, the point I want to make is that psychoanalytic theory, that disgusting philosophy, has been incapable of becoming aware of this simple fact. Psychoanalysts claim that all of people's actions, including mystical experiences, are nothing more than transformed sexual energies. Psychoanalysts, or we might even say materialists in general, take sexuality as their starting point and explain all other human phenomena as metamorphoses of

100

sexuality. I have already pointed out how in Freud's theory everything that happens in a person's life is explained in terms of transformed sexuality. For example, that babies suck on pacifiers is explained as an expression of infantile sexuality, and so forth.

But what is the truth of the matter? In reality, my friends, any other human daily activity is more spiritual than sexual activity, and to arrive at the right perspective on this subject, we have to look at things the other way around. Any attempt to explain what people do by dragging in sexuality and eroticism is completely wrong. The right way of looking at things is to explain sexuality as the transformation of higher human activities into their lowest earthly form.

Since I have been forced to mention the ghastly claims of the psychoanalysts because they are an unavoidable phenomenon of our times, let us take a look at one of the worst of them, namely their contention that the loving childhood relationship of a boy to his mother or a girl to her father is actually a sexual relationship. Psychoanalysts claim that a girl's feelings for her father and a boy's for his mother are sexual feelings, and that boys always view their father as a rival and are unconsciously jealous of him; girls, so they say, are similarly jealous of their mother. This is one of the most terrible of the distortions psychoanalysts have perpetrated. In their writings, as you know, they have even used this assumption as the basis for explaining certain literary works such as the story of Oedipus.[2]

In looking for the right perspective on this subject, we need to ask how adult sexuality develops. As we have seen, it comes about through something spiritual sinking down into matter. Our adult sexuality comes about through the descent of something that was spiritual when we were children. The correct approach is to avoid getting anything not specifically sexual mixed up with sexuality, either consciously or unconsciously, and to realize that sexuality is not yet present in children. Only when we are fully aware of all the ramifications of this can we find the right perspective on the matter. This is an extremely important point with regard to the education of children, because all kinds of things can go wrong if childish mischief is automatically interpreted as premature sexuality. All kinds of things other than sexuality can be the reason for children misbehaving. Claiming that there is already a sexual side to a child's character is just about the same as insisting that tomorrow's rainy weather is already inherent in today.

By now you will have realized what we are dealing with here—the perspective that has been applied is totally upside down and backward. Coming to such a distorted perspective does not happen naturally, but only by forcing the issue and arbitrarily dragging in our instincts. The whole psychoanalytic approach is tinged with the lowest human instincts; it turns the world upside down. Such an interpretation of the mother-daughter or father-son relationship can only come about if the researcher's subjective instincts get mixed up with the objective course of the investigation. Consequently, in this instance (providing we go about it with all due exactitude), it is perfectly all right to apply expressions usually reserved for subjective human actions. While it would be foolish to apply subjective expressions to a legitimate and objective science, it is possible to do so in this case without relinquishing the objectivity of our point of view.

Just imagine someone believes that the hands of a clock are turned by little demons sitting inside—we would call that foolish, of course. Clocks are mechanical devices; there are no little devils inside. Reacting to it objectively, however, we would never say that the person who attributes the clock's functioning to demons is insulting the clock. But when psychoanalysts attribute this sort of sexuality to children, instinctual subjectivity invades their theory. Then it is justified to use subjective expressions and say that the psychoanalytic theory insults human nature. We must make an effort to be truthful and call a spade a spade. In our materialistic world, a number of people have made it their task to cultivate a theory that demeans not only individuals, but human nature in general, to the extent that their whole scientific theory is nothing more than a compilation of insults. When a sufficient number of people realize that this is happening, we will start to see psychoanalytic theory for exactly what it's worth. Then we won't be merely peddling with words any more, but will be able to see things as they are. That's how we can come to clarity on this issue.

Only after we have completely understood everything we have discussed today can our understanding be allowed to lead to name-calling. When we call psychoanalysis a smutty theory, that obviously really is name-calling; however, our insight into the objective fact of the matter is what compels us to call it by this name. After all, it would not be right for the criticism to come from the same kind of subjective instincts as the theory itself.

The unique thing about spiritual science, however, is that an apparently abstract theory is transformed into justified feelings and reactions. Those who have gone through a real struggle to understand what psychoanalysis actually is can freely call it a smutty theory without losing their objectivity. It is as objective to call psychoanalysis a smutty theory as it is to say that canvas is white and charcoal black. It is objective terminology derived from true insight into human nature in its totality.

The purpose of our spiritual scientific philosophy is to deepen our concepts, and not only our concepts but our whole character, my friends. If we say that a Society intended as the vehicle for this philosophy must be a living organism, then we must also be able to see how the emotions expressed within the context of the Society also develop out of this spiritual scientific philosophy, so that even a radical expression such as "smutty theory" can only be applied when it is firmly rooted in spiritual science and when no personal instincts play a part in its use.

I am sure we will soon find an opportunity for further discussion of related matters.

PART TWO

Documentation
on the Dornach Crisis of 1915

with two addresses by Rudolf Steiner
and editorial comments by
Hella Wiesberger and Ulla Trapp

I

The Protagonists

IN 1913 on the hill in Dornach near Basel, Switzerland, construction had begun on the building then known as the *Johannesbau* and later to be called the *Goetheanum*, the central headquarters of the anthroposophical movement. Members of the Anthroposophical Society from all parts of the world had been called upon to work on the building, and they were joined by a growing number of others who moved to Dornach, either permanently or temporarily, on their own initiative. Thus a unique center of anthroposophical activity developed in Dornach, a center that was, understandably enough, burdened with the shortcomings and problems unavoidable in such a group.

In the summer of 1914, these difficulties escalated when World War I broke out, since people from many different nations, including those at war, had to work together and get along with each other. Isolation from the rest of the world and, last but not least, both local and more widespread opposition to the building and the people it attracted, further complicated the situation. In spite of all obstacles, however, the building continued to grow under the artistic leadership of Rudolf Steiner, who was well-loved as a teacher and felt by all to be a bulwark of constancy. But in the summer of 1915 all this changed as a result of incidents that threatened to test the

Dornach group, and thus the Anthroposophical Society as a whole, to the breaking point.

Rudolf Steiner's marriage to Marie von Sivers at Christmas of 1914 had provoked not only general gossip, but also some bizarre mystical behavior on the part of a member named Alice Sprengel.[1] Heinrich Goesch (see below) and his wife Gertrud seized upon her strange ideas and made use of them in personal attacks on Rudolf Steiner. Since this was done publicly in the context of the Society, Rudolf Steiner asked that the Society itself resolve the case. This resulted in weeks of debate, at the end of which all three were expelled from the Society. Rudolf and Marie Steiner did not take part either in the debates or in the decision to rescind their membership.

The documents that follow reconstruct the events of the case in the sequence in which they occurred.

Alice Sprengel (b. 1871 in Scotland, d. 1949 in Bern, Switzerland) had joined the Theosophical Society in Munich in the summer of 1902, at a time when Rudolf Steiner had not yet become General Secretary for Germany. She joined the German Section a few years later. In a notice issued by the *Vorstand* of the Anthroposophical Society in the fall of 1915 informing members about the case, Miss Sprengel is described as having undergone unusual suffering in her childhood. At the time of her entry into the Society, she still impressed people as being very dejected. In addition, she was unemployed at that time and outwardly in very unfortunate circumstances. For that reason, efforts were made to help her

Marie Steiner, then Marie von Sivers, sponsored her involvement in the Munich drama festival in 1907 and arranged for her to be financially supported by members in Munich. In order to help her find a means of supporting herself in line with her artistic abilities, Rudolf Steiner advised her on making symbolic jewelry and the like for members of the Society. It was also made possible for her to make the move to Dornach in 1914. She, however, interpreted this generous assistance to mean that she had a significant mission to fulfill within the Society. Having been given the role of Theodora in Rudolf Steiner's mystery dramas fed her delusions with regard to her mission, as did the fact that toward the end of the year 1911, in conjunction with the project to construct a building to house the mystery dramas, Rudolf Steiner had made an attempt to found a "Society for Theosophical Art and Style" in which she had been nominated as "keeper of the seal" because of her work as an artist. She imagined having lived through important incarnations and even believed herself to be the inspirer of Rudolf Steiner's spiritual teachings. In addition, having been asked to play Theodora gave rise to the delusion that she had received a symbolic promise of marriage from Rudolf Steiner, and she then suffered a breakdown as a result of Rudolf Steiner's marriage to Marie von Sivers at Christmas 1914. Her letters to Rudolf Steiner and Marie Steiner, reproduced below, clearly reveal that she was deeply upset.

Letter from Alice Sprengel to Rudolf Steiner
(undated; received December 25, 1914. Cf. p. 159.)

"Seven years now have passed,"[2] Dr. Steiner, since you appeared to my inner vision and said to me, "I am the one you have spent your life waiting for; I am the one for whom the powers of destiny intended you."

You saw the struggles and doubts this experience occasioned in me; you knew that in the end my conviction was unshakable—yes, so it is. And you waited for my soul to open and for me to speak about this. Yet I remained silent, because my heart was broken. Long before I learned of theosophy, but also much more recently, I had had many experiences that made me say, "I willingly accept whatever suffering life brings me, no matter how hard it may be. After all, I have been shown by the spirit that it cannot be different." But this is something that seems to go beyond the original plan of destiny; I lack the strength to bear it, and so it kills something in me, destroys forces I should once have possessed. These experiences were mostly instances of people deliberately abusing my confidence, and all in the name of love. But I had the feeling that this was not only my own fault; it seemed as if the will of destiny was inflicting more on me than I could bear.

I had some vague idea of why that might be so. Once, some years ago, I heard a voice within me saying, "There are beings in the spiritual world whose work requires that human beings sustain hope, but they have no interest in seeing these hopes fulfilled—on the contrary." At that point I was not fully aware of what we were later to hear about the mystery of premature death, of goals not achieved, and so forth.

Then, however, I bore within me a wish and a hope that seemed like a proclamation from the spiritual world. This wish and this hope had made it possible for me to bear the unbearable; they worked in me with such tremendous force that they carried me along with them. My soul was in such a condition, however, that it could neither relinquish them nor tolerate their fulfillment, or, to put it better, it could not live up to what their fulfillment would have demanded of it. Thus I could not come to clarity on what the above-mentioned experience meant for me as an earthly human being. Neither the teaching nor the teacher was enough to revive my soul; that could only be done by a human being capable of greater love than any other and thus capable of compensating for a greater lack of love.

I can no longer remain silent; it speaks in me and forces me to speak. Years ago I begged you for advice, asked for enlightenment, and your words gave me hope and comfort. I am grateful for that, but today I would no longer be able to bear it. Why did you say to me recently that I looked well, that I should persevere? Did you think I was already aware of the step you are taking now, and that I had already "gotten over it"? I was as far from that as ever.

In conclusion, I ask that you let Miss von Sivers read this letter.

Alice Sprengel

* * *

Letter from Alice Sprengel to Rudolf Steiner

Arlesheim
February 3, 1915

Dear Dr. Steiner,

This will probably be my last letter to you; I will never turn to you again, neither in speaking nor in writing. I only want to tell you that I see no way out for myself; I am at my wits' end. As the weeks gone by have showed me, it is inconceivable that time will alleviate or wipe out anything that has happened; it will only bring to light what is hidden. Until now I have more or less managed to conceal how I feel, but I will not be able to do so indefinitely. I feel a melancholy settling in on me; being together with others and feeling their attentiveness is a torment to me, but I also cannot tolerate being alone for any length of time. I feel that everything that was to develop in me and flow into our movement through me has been buried alive.

My life stretches ahead of me, but it is devoid of any breath of air that makes life possible. And yet, in the darkest hour of my existence, I feel condemned to live—but my soul will be dead. Desolation and numbness will alternate with bouts of pain. I cannot imagine how the tragedy will end. It is likely, though, that I will show some signs of sorrow in weeks to come, and it may well be that I will say and do things that will surprise me as much as anyone else. I do not have the feeling that my words will arouse any echo in you. I feel as if I were talking to a picture. Since that time early on in those seven years when I stood bodily in front of you and you appeared to me as the embodiment of the figure that had been revealed to my inner

111

vision, you have become unreal to me. Then, your voice sounded as sweet and comforting as my own hopes. You restored my soul with mysterious hints and promises that were so often contradicted in the course of events. And when my soul wanted to unfold under that radiant gaze of yours in which I could read that you knew what had happened to me, something looked at me out of your eyes, crying "This is a temptation."

The most terrible thing was to have what stood before me in visible human form become unreal to me. And yet, I had the feeling that there was something real behind all this. I do not know what power makes your essential being a reality for me. You know that I have struggled for my faith and will continue to do so as long as there is a glimmer of life in me. You also know how I have pleaded with that Being whose light and teachings you must bring to those who suffer the terrible fate of being human, pleaded that whatever guilt may flow on my account may not disturb you in your mission, and I have the feeling that I have been heard. Nevertheless, the shadow of what has happened to me will fall across your path, just as it will darken my future earthly lives. That shadow will also fall across the continued existence of our movement and upon the destiny of our building. If the mystery dramas are ever performed again, you will have to have another Theodora, and since I will *never* be able to come to terms with what has happened, the very doors of the temple are closed to me in future. I wonder if, under these circumstances, there will ever again.... I do not need to finish the sentence.

I sense that, on an occult level, this is a terrible state of affairs. Is there no way out?

Only a miracle can help in this case.

I am well aware that deliverance is possible, and if it were not to come, it would be terrible, and not only for me.

Let me tell you a story by way of conclusion, the story of the "sœur gardienne."[3]

During the preparations for the plays during the summer of 1913, I noticed that you were not satisfied with me, and when it was all over I felt like a sick person who knows the doctor has given up on her. That feeling never left me from then on, and I could tell you of many instances, especially in recent months, when I felt a deathly chill come over me although your words actually sounded encouraging. The feeling grew stronger whenever I encountered anyone who knew what lay ahead. Why do I feel as if someone had slapped me in the face? Don't they all look as if they were part of a plot? That's what came to mind on many occasions, but I was relatively cheerful then and put it out of my mind. But all this is just a digression.

Two summers ago, shortly before the rehearsals began, I read *La Sœur Gardienne*. I had always assumed that Miss von Sivers would play the title role. On reading it, however, I began to doubt that the role would suit her; in fact, it seemed to me that she would not even want to play that part. And then I noticed how the figure came alive within me—it spoke, it moved in me. It was my role. If only I were allowed to play it! I saw what it would mean to me, and it was too beautiful to be true. Then invisible eyes looked at me, and I heard, "They will not give you that part, so resign yourself." In my experience, that voice had always been correct. In view of the existing situation, I said to myself, "Dr. Steiner knows as well as I do that I had this experience; he must have good reasons for arranging things this way in spite of it—and as far as Miss von Sivers is concerned, I must have been mistaken—the whole thing must simply be another one of the incomprehensible disappointments that run like a red thread through my life."

My soul collapsed; I behaved as calmly as I could, but that did not seem to be good enough. Your behavior as well as Miss von Sivers' was totally incomprehensible to me. They were looking everywhere for someone, anyone, to take the title role, and no one seemed to think of me; anyone else seemed more desirable. And yet people were making comments about how strange it was that I had nothing to do in that play. I held back, because at one point I was really afraid I would have to play a different role. Performances have been more or less the only occasions in my life where I could breathe freely, so to speak, where I could give of myself. But that was only true when I played parts that lived in me, like Theodora and Persephone. But when a role didn't sit well with me, it increased the pressure I was living under for quite some time. That is why I was not as unconcerned about these things as others might be; for me it was a matter of life and death. In the midst of all this tension something befell me that I had already experienced countless times before in many different situations and against which I have always been defenseless. My soul crumples as soon as it happens. Once again, "it" looked at me and said, "This is a lesson for you!" (or sometimes it said "a test" or "an ordeal").

I felt the effects in my soul of countless experiences, repeated daily, hourly, going back to my earliest childhood. I do not know why my surroundings have always been tempted to participate wrongfully in my inner life. Only here and only very recently have I been able to ward this off, but it has forced me into complete isolation. What my foster parents, teachers, playmates, friends, and even strangers used to do to see what kind of a face I would make or to guess at how I would react! And much more than that. As I said, these experiences were so frequent that I could not deal with them; they suffocated me. Mostly I took it all calmly, thinking they didn't know any better. Now, however, in the situation I described, these semi-conscious memories played a trick on me—and I was overcome by anger. And then this summer, a year later, I had to relive the whole thing. And it occurred to me that I should have told you about what went before it.

As I said, those words "This is a lesson for you" always made me stiffen and freeze. When I look back on my life, it seems as if a devilish wisdom had foreseen all the possibilities life would bring to me in these last few years, and as if this intelligence had done its utmost to make me unfit for them. I could watch it at work, and yet was powerless to do anything. Much could be said about why that happened. But nothing in my own soul or in any single soul could ever help me over this abyss. Only the spark leaping from soul to soul, the spark that is so weak now, so very weak, can make the miracle happen now....

February 5

I have just read over what I wrote, and now I wonder, is it really all right for everything to happen as I described? That is how it would have to happen if everything stays as it is now. But don't we all three feel how destiny stands between us? Can it really be that there is one among us who does not know what has to happen next? That will bring many things to light; the course of events to come depends on what had been one person's secret. This is truly a test, but not only for me. What was hidden shall be revealed.

I still have one thing to say to you, my teacher and guide: even though the tempter looks out of your eyes, there have been times when I experienced with a shudder that what was revealed to me also meant something to you, something that has not been given its due. However, this must happen and will happen—you know that well, and so does

The Keeper of the Seal

* * *

Excerpt from a letter from Alice Sprengel to Marie Steiner (undated; received on August 21, 1915. Cf. p. 139 and p. 160.)

I know that people who have "occult experiences" are a calamity as far as the people in positions of responsibility in our movement are concerned, and understandably so, but still, that is what our movement is there for—to come to grips with things like that.

The relationship between you and Dr. Steiner is not the point right now; no, it is the relationship between you and myself. However, your civil marriage unleashed a disaster for me, one that I had feared and seen coming for years—not in its actual course of events, you understand, but in its nature and severity. That is to say, for years I had seen something developing between my teacher and me, something to which we can indeed apply what we have heard in the last few days, though not for the first time. It has a will of its own and laws of its own and cannot be exorcised with any clever magic word. As I said, I had sufficient self-knowledge to know what had to come if nothing happened to prevent it.

Three years ago, like a sick person seeking out a physician, I asked Dr. Steiner for a consultation. There was something very sad I had to say during that interview, and I have had to say it frequently since then: Although I could follow his teachings, I could not understand anything of what affected me directly or of what happened to me. I must omit what brought me to the point of saying this, since I do not know how much you know about my background and biography. I was not able to express my need, and Dr. Steiner made it clear that he did not want to hear about it. The following summer, however, we were graced with the opportunity to perform *The Guardian of the Threshold*; in it a conversation takes place between Strader and Theodora, a conversation that reflected in the most delicate way the very thing that was oppressing me. Perhaps Dr. Steiner did not "intend" anything of the sort; nevertheless, it is a fact. Perhaps it was meant as an attempt at healing. I do not understand....

* * *

The next letter, written by an Englishwoman who was living at the Goetheanum at the time, characterizes Alice Sprengel from a different point of view:

116

Letter from Mary Peet to Alice Sprengel[4]

Arlesheim,
October 1915

Dear Miss Sprengel,

I cannot let the time pass without writing to tell you how greatly shocked I am at your disgraceful behavior to Doctor Steiner—and also to Mrs. Steiner.

I have truly always thought of you as a rather delicate and hysterical looking [*sic*] person, but I little imagined to what depths your evidently hysterical nature could lead you.

Your illusive hope of becoming a prominent person in our society not having been realized has been too much of a disappointment for your nature. This kind of thing happens every day, in that disappointed young women fall into all sorts of hysterical conditions, which give rise to all sorts of fantastical dreams. In this case the most holy things have been mixed with false illusions arising from much vanity, self-pride, and the desire for greatness!

To one who pictures herself to be the reincarnation of David, and of the Virgin Mary, very little can be said, for if one starts with such suppositions, one necessarily places oneself almost beyond the pale of reason and logic.

A dog will not bite the hand that has fed it for years—you have not shown the fidelity of a dog in that you have turned all your hatred and spite against the one who has given you all that has brought life into your existence, both spiritually and physically, for you have been beholden to him and his friends for your subsistence.

And now, because you are thoroughly disappointed, you have tried and are trying your best to injure him with every subtle untruth and insinuation, engendered by those thoughts which have entered your imaginative brain.

Doctor Steiner is beloved, revered, and respected; his life is

117

an example to all. He has been able through his power of logic and clear and right thinking to feed us with the bread of Wisdom and Life, and has truly been a Light-bringer to us all.

I implore you to listen to reason before it is too late! Try to examine yourself for one hour and perceive the *cause* of all the fearful self-deception from which you are suffering. Beware of the awful figure of HATE, called up by your jealousy and consequent disappointment!

You *cannot undo* the past, but you *can try* to redeem the lost opportunities you have had by refraining from showing more and more clearly the picture that many can see—to which you are apparently quite blind up till now—namely, that of jealous woman suffering from ingratitude, disappointment, and hysterical illusions!

O Man! Know Thyself!

Truly,

[signed Mary Peet]

* * *

Heinrich Goesch (b. 1880 in Rostock, d. 1930 in Konstanz) was a man of many talents and interests who was already a Ph.D. and LL.D. at age twenty. His name also appeared once in December 1900 on the list of those present at a meeting of the Berlin literary society *Die Kommenden*. Financial support from parents and relatives enabled him to lead a life that allowed him to pursue numerous interests. Except for the last years of his life, when he lectured on art at the Dresden Academy of Arts and Crafts, he had never actually practiced a profession, presumably for reasons of health. According to a report by the psychiatrist Friedrich Husemann, Goesch had suffered from a very early age from epilepsy or seizure substitutes (absences). An expert witness reports having experienced one of Goesch's heaviest seizures.[5]

Goesch had come into contact with psychoanalysis in 1908 or 1909 while living with his wife (a cousin of Käthe Kollwitz) and his brother Paul, a painter, in Niederpoyritz near Dresden, where they were engaged in studying architecture, aesthetics, and philosophy. Paul Fechter, a journalist who was a friend of the Goeschs at that time, reports the following in his memoirs:[6]

Such was the world that greeted the dawning of psychoanalysis. One day Heinrich Goesch made the acquaintance of one of its earliest adepts, the son of a professor in Graz, who had made the teachings of Sigmund Freud, which at that time had not yet been widely popularized, the basis of his whole life. Goesch took him along to Niederpoyritz, where in endless nightly sessions the young doctor initiated the two brothers into the secrets of the new doctrine. As a result, Heinrich and Paul Goesch, consistent and logical in all their intellectual pursuits, were not content with the theory, but set about putting it into practice. They not only listened to what their guest had to offer, they tried it out on themselves and anything else they could get their hands on. They analyzed themselves and others and staged complex-resolutions by night until Niederpoyritz rebelled and their reputation rivaled that of young Schlegel in Jena.

All that would have made no difference; rumors get started and then fade away again. The effect on Paul Goesch, however, was disastrous—his thin-skinned psyche cracked under these experiments. Analysis, it seems, had eliminated certain inhibitions he needed in order to maintain a secure hold on life. Shortly after the doctor's visit, he entered a mental hospital for the first time....

The "doctor" whose name Fechter does not reveal was Otto Gross, private lecturer in psychopathology at the University of Graz and one of Freud's first pupils. Unlike Freud, who used psychoanalysis simply as a method of medical treatment, Gross,

119

by applying it in social and political contexts as well, tried to make it the underlying basis of everyday life. His efforts eventually brought him into conflict with all existing social structures. As a drug addict, he became a patient of C. G. Jung at the Burghoelzli in Zurich and in that capacity played a certain role in the professional disagreements between Jung and Freud. Later, at the instigation of his father, Hans Gross (professor of criminology at Graz), he was declared legally incompetent and spent most of the rest of his life in mental hospitals.[7]

In his obituary of Heinrich Goesch, Fechter has this to say about Goesch's relationship to psychoanalysis:

> When Otto Gross first introduced him to the as yet relatively unknown psychoanalytic method of Sigmund Freud, Heinrich Goesch recognized it immediately as a means of extending his personal experience into unfathomed depths. He took up this new subject passionately, not as a theoretical, conceptual, or abstract object of study and experience, but plunging with his whole being and all the strength he possessed into this stream that opened up before him and led into new depths. He did not study psychoanalysis, he experienced it through and through, making himself the object of his own analysis, descending into the shocks and ecstasies of the darkness that opened up in front of him with a total disregard for how it might affect his everyday existence. At once, he began to pull the theory out of the realm of science and into his immediate personal experience. It was a very dangerous experiment....[8]

Goesch became acquainted with Rudolf Steiner's anthroposophy around 1910. Shortly thereafter, he became a member of the German Section of the Theosophical Society, led at that point by Rudolf Steiner as General Secretary. He had been recommended by the physician Max Asch, who wrote to Rudolf Steiner on April 27, 1910:[9]

For the last two weeks or so, I have been involved in a lively and personal exchange of ideas with a Mr. Heinrich Goesch, Ph.D., who seems to me predestined for occult training. He is one of the most highly gifted people I have ever met, and about one year ago had unusual inner experiences that occurred as part of a state of ecstasy lasting about a week, which leads me to assume that his case would be of particular interest to you, too. He has recently immersed himself in the study of your works (*Theosophy*, *An Outline of Occult Science*, etc.), and the unbelievable quickness with which he grasps these things leads me to suspect that he has undergone some form of occult schooling in an earlier incarnation—apparently a specifically Christian one, given the nature of his ecstatic experiences. Mr. Goesch will attend your lecture tomorrow evening; if you wish, I will introduce him to you. He wants to become a member of the Theosophical Society immediately.

The lecture in question took place on April 28, 1910, in the Berlin House of Architects. Its title was "Error and Mental Disorder."[10] On April 30, 1910, Asch wrote to Rudolf Steiner again:

Heinrich Goesch, Ph.D., about whom I wrote to you, would be very grateful if you would find an opportunity to speak with him soon. He would like to attend your lectures in Hamburg, since they are related to an area he has researched with particular interest in the last few years. Therefore, he would like to become a member of the Theosophical Society as soon as possible. Mr. Goesch lives in Charlottenburg....

A short time after Heinrich Goesch and his wife Gertrud became members, the construction of a building to serve as its central headquarters became a focal point of the Society's activity. Goesch was very interested in architecture and in 1912 made some suggestions about the design of the building. This interest, it seems, was also what led him to come in the spring of

1914 to Dornach, where work on the *Johannesbau* (first Goetheanum) had begun in fall of 1913.

These facts from the biography of Goesch, who, as Paul Fechter puts it, displayed "a personal and unique combination of logic and mysticism," make it somewhat understandable why he would jump into the Sprengel case with typical passionate energy. According to the psychiatrist Friedrich Husemann, epileptics characteristically combine egocentricity with a disproportionate sensitivity to personal affront and a tendency to complain. On the basis of these changes in their affective life, it is easy for them to develop delusions, and a certain affinity must have developed between Goesch's delusions and those of Alice Sprengel. Goesch formulated his thoughts in a long and elaborate letter (dated August 19, 1915) to Rudolf Steiner, who read it to the Dornach circle on August 21, 1915, in place of his usual Saturday evening lecture.

II

Address by Rudolf Steiner

DORNACH, AUGUST 21, 1915

MY ADDRESS this evening represents a break in our current series; its subject is quite different from yesterday's.[1] This morning I received a letter, and I feel compelled, even obligated, to bring it to the attention of each individual member of the Anthroposophical Society. I will explain my reasons after I read you the letter.

Letter from Heinrich and Gertrud Goesch to Rudolf Steiner

Dornach
August 19, 1915

Dear Dr. Steiner:

Alongside the work dedicated to the good within your activity in our spiritual movement, I have noticed certain behaviors that serve evil purposes. On the good side, I am grateful for the esoteric knowledge and teachings you have imparted to us, for the mystery dramas you have given us, for the introduction of eurythmy, and for the art of the *Johannesbau*. In these contexts,

I continue to recognize you as an envoy of the great white lodge and am filled with profound gratitude to you and to anything you do that is devoted to the good.

However, I perceive the way you cultivate relationships between yourself and other members of our spiritual movement as serving evil purposes, and I see this behavior as gravely endangering our movement. The relationships you create between yourself and other members turn the others into merely parts of yourself rather than independent spiritual entities alongside you. You only appear to act as a human being among equals. In actuality, you scorn any truly human connection and presume to intervene in the lives of others in a way that belongs only to the gods and not to any modern human being.

In this way, you create an anti-Christian relationship between yourself and the other members of our spiritual movement. These people have readied themselves to meet great spiritual teachings in our time, but you are making them poorer than the poorest materialists out there, who in spite of their distorted Christianity that has turned into its exact opposite are still able to develop a strong I. If it goes on like this, however, your followers will eventually fall prey to black magic as a result of the constant weakening of their I through how you behave toward them.

There have already been instances of highly respected members substituting a reliance on your word for reliance on the truth; they cut off any criticism of any part of your work, objecting that your critics would be placing themselves above you. They feel that putting oneself above you is such an act of wanton temerity as to be out of the question, and that with their objection the issue is resolved once and for all. The members are not to blame for erroneous ideas like this—you are. In your concern to promulgate ever more of your teachings, you have neglected to cultivate the attitude among your pupils that as Christians, individuals must put themselves not only below any other person, but also above any other; not only are the least of

124

our fellow human beings of irreplaceable value to us in their most profound depths of being, but also the least of us carry responsibility for the most advanced and must oppose their errors. Your own teachings have strengthened me in this conviction. In real life, however, you apply a number of means that work counter to this Christian ideal of human community.

I will now discuss two of these means in detail so that the thrust of my contentions becomes clearer.

It is a fact that you have developed the habit of making promises and not keeping them. No one will maintain that you do not have a sufficiently clear view of the future, or that you are too weak to carry out your original intentions, either of which would constitute a certain justification for failing to keep promises. No, this is a case of deliberately causing disappointment. Since the promises were unsolicited and made at your own initiative, it is also a case of deliberate intervention into someone else's life in order do something that is by rights reserved for destiny. A disappointment that comes to us through karma has a direct and beneficial effect on our development. In contrast, a disappointment deliberately arranged for us by another person is at the very least a heavy blow, and if our confidence in the person delivering the blow is not shaken, it also constitutes a weakening of our I. The difference is the same as the difference between meeting an accidental death in a burning building and death by burning at the stake, premeditated by others.

Because of their trust in you, recipients of such a promise who are waiting for it to be kept get into a state of tension and uncertainty; meanwhile you are able to calmly survey their gradually increasing disappointment. Once the people in question have realized that the promise is not going to be kept, they will not take your word seriously in the future and thus will distance themselves from you, at least to some extent. However, since on the whole they continue to put their trust in you, they will lose all standards for the sanctity of giving one's word, and may perhaps begin to act as you do. As a result, they are dependent on you in a humanly unworthy fashion and will try to affect others in the same way you do.

Alternatively, people may respond in one of the three following ways: First, because of the confidence they have in you, they may assume that there must be a deep occult meaning behind the way you act. They will conclude that there can be profound occult reasons that permit or even obligate someone to make promises without intending to keep them. Occasionally we even meet people whose emotions are so confused that they admire that kind of behavior and take it as a sign of something superhuman. It is evident, however, that nothing in this world can authorize a modern human being to make promises without intending to keep them. Causing disappointment is something reserved for the gods who direct our karma.

This sort of conceptual confusion is all the more dangerous for a student of esotericism because modern spiritual science appeals to our healthy capacity for discernment, which is undermined by things like this. In a most unfortunate fashion, your word displaces the truth; the thought "I must not place myself above him" displaces the realization that you have done something evil. The human dignity of these people crumbles away bit by bit, and they turn into spiritually dependent tools in your hands.

The second possibility for those whose trust has been betrayed is that in order to be able to maintain their confidence in you, the people in question never let themselves become fully conscious of the fact that you never had any intention of keeping the promises you made to them. As a way out, they take your not keeping promises as a new revelation of a being they do not experience as really human and cannot hold responsible as they would a human being. This point of view is in fact already represented within the Society and is leading to your becoming ever more shadowlike as a human being.

The third and final possibility is that some people will choose the radical way out, forgetting the fact that a promise of some kind was ever made. This, too, robs people of a bit of their I. As a result, your coworkers in our spiritual movement will be shadows whose I is weakened, rather than independent individuals. You yourself, however, are the one to blame for all this.

A second example of the evil nature of your behavior is your refusal to accept any criticism of people working in our movement. On occasion, you have implied that any such criticism stems from negative emotions. This is a false assumption. I am not talking about malicious or destructive criticism. Many of our members, out of their sincere sense of responsibility, are capable of constructive criticism, and that is what I am talking about. The only possible reason for avoiding such criticism would be knowing that people in positions of responsibility are unfit for their jobs. In our modern age, people are meant to come together out of their own free will and freely create the kind of hierarchy and order necessary for us to accomplish what we have to do, and a certain amount of constructive mutual criticism is our only guarantee of success. In fact, the only way a true, natural, and appropriate hierarchical order can come about nowadays is if this kind of criticism is allowed to work.

If people who have been criticized do not choose to take action on justified accusations—and in fact they are morally obliged to actively seek criticism—they must give up their positions in the hierarchy so that the truth can triumph. Their superiors should not protect people like that by acting as if everything were going fine. This is what our modern age requires. However, if at any level in the hierarchical order mistakes are not criticized but tolerated and allowed to persist, we are only creating a false hierarchy that is based, not on real human capabilities and relationships, but on fiction—a fiction that is maintained only through further wrongdoing. Once again, the result is a lack of humanity and Christianity in our relationships in general, and once again you are to blame. In the organization of our Society as it has gradually developed under your guidance, the strengths of the members are usurped to the advantage of yourself and perhaps of certain other people prominent in this false hierarchy. Meanwhile, the Society's affairs are being mismanaged.

Personal oversensitivity on the part of those being criticized is something that needs to be eliminated; you might give a lecture about this sometime. As a general rule, especially if it comes at the right moment, criticism can take a stimulating and gratifying form and be free of any personal bitterness, so that its thorns are removed and the recipient can be glad to receive help in resolving the issue. The nervousness and animosity so prevalent among the critics spring in part from the justified feeling that even the most objective criticism will not be heeded, but will be looked at askance and disregarded. A truly superior person has no reason to fear criticism; true superiority can stand the test of even the most pointed criticism. In the event that people attempt to offer criticism out of a sense of responsibility but are not really able to grasp the facts of the case, those people can usually be made to see their misunderstanding sooner or later without any undue waste of time.

At the moment, I am not talking about a case like this one, where the criticism has already developed into a well-founded rejection of an entire self-contained system confronting me. In this case, no amount of postponement would make any difference. If in a specific instance, however, a person I myself recognize as superior—not simply someone who, for some unknown reason, is my superior in a false hierarchy—points out that I do not yet fully understand the case in question, I will gladly defer my criticism until the case can be considered closed. Under your influence, however, the principle at work in our spiritual movement is that any such criticism should be withheld indefinitely—until the facts of the case have been forgotten. And this principle applies not only to certain specific cases, but to all such instances. This is not only wrong and harmful to everyone, it also undermines our discernment, on which so much depends.

Once again, I have to point out the inherent contradiction between spiritual science's appeal to people's healthy power of judgment and the fact that in most instances in our movement, this power of judgment must be subordinated to incomprehensible reasons for measures being taken. You must admit, however, that at this point in time, two thousand years after Christ, people possess certain standards that all individuals can apply and must also allow to be applied to themselves, if they are not to be utterly lost. There are certainly a sufficient number of closed cases that really are subject to our judgment. The mere fact that a person feels compelled to think about a particular case usually suggests that he or she is capable of achieving some clarity in the matter, though not necessarily without help.

As things stand at the moment, our members are constantly expending a considerable portion of their spiritual energy on the useless task of seeking out hidden wisdom-filled motives for the evil behavior of yourself and your highest colleagues, while you stand by, calmly observing this waste of effort. Or, in order not to lose faith in you, these people have to decide to repress these truth-seeking forces in themselves and thus fall prey to partial stupefaction. What happens with these forces then? What a horrible thought to pursue! In any case, you represent a great focal point of forces of which individuals are merely the instruments, to be used as you choose for incomprehensible ends. There is no question in our movement of real interaction taking place between complete human beings, interaction in which each one is allowed to contribute his or her best. You are not a friend to all the members; your whole attitude rejects lively friendly relationships. In truth, for many people, you are the greatest enemy they have ever encountered.

All these things I have described are not only objectively evil, they also directly contradict the teachings you promulgate. It is from you that I learned the reasons that lead me to reject the way you act. As time goes on, you give an ever stronger impression of acting on your connection to the Christ impulse only in your lectures; outside the lectures, you embrace impulses that are quite the opposite. In parts, it already seems to me as if your teaching has been somewhat influenced by what you practice in real life—not the content of your teachings, but their formal structure. In their structure, certain sentences make promises that are then not kept and can only serve the purpose of subjecting the reader to fruitless thought and work. (See "Gedanken während der Zeit des Krieges.")[2] If people try to explain this by saying that you, like any other human being, may have changed your mind over the course of time, you reject this as irksome criticism (Preface to *Riddles of Philosophy*, last paragraph).[3] Both these passages, by the way, clearly show a change in style verging on the incomprehensible.

The kind of interpersonal attitude you create not only contradicts your teachings; your behavior also contradicts what you yourself demand of spiritual teachers in the modern age. Such teachers should appeal only to people's consciousness. Their self-chosen obligation toward their students is to never exercise any magical influence on the students' subconscious that the latter have not consented to or cannot control. You, however, are doing this incessantly through the behavior I described and through other occult means. For you, every handshake, every friendly conversation becomes a means of cultivating these false relationships. The bliss that fills the members after meeting with you is not the bliss of the communion of saints, but a merely Luciferic-Ahrimanic one. You, not the members themselves, are to blame for this. You even try to use these handshakes and friendly conversations to pull members back into the fold against their will once they have recognized the falsity of the relationships you try to create. I have perceived with certainty that you exercise undue influence on your followers in this way.

In the modern age, when any uncontrollable influence on the subconscious of others must be avoided, it is not enough to simply give lectures or introduce new spirituality. In addition, the life you lead together with the other members of our movement must be governed by Christian impulses; your relationships with your followers must become like those of Benedictus, so beautifully portrayed in your fourth mystery drama. In fact, now that we have received so much in the way of teachings, developing such relationships is the much more urgent obligation.

When I ask myself how it can possibly be that you whose task it was to proclaim these teachings can act in ways directly counter to them, I can conceive of two possible answers. On the one hand, I can guess at the reasons why the great white lodge might have had to choose a person who is not yet completely Christianized for this task, and in your capacity as teacher I still accept you as the envoy of the lodge. On the other hand, it seems to me that your most profound motivation is by no means actively evil, although what I have had to say might be erroneously interpreted to imply that. No, it is simply a too one-sided interest in renewing these teachings in a way appropriate to our times, and above all a fear of real life. By avoiding and obstructing real life and by creating substitutes for it, however, you allow an evil force to develop. In this, I see the greatest danger to our spiritual movement and to yourself.

Fully Christian occultists can never rest content with simply passing on teachings; they must also enter into a life partnership with their students. True relationships from person to person in the Christian sense require each one of us to be an open book to all others to the extent their individual strength permits. All people should give themselves completely to their fellows to whatever extent the latter can receive them. This should be the basis of any modern hierarchy. Those higher up in the hierarchy must turn to those beneath them with whatever they have to give. What you practice, however, is anti-Christian and just the opposite. Whenever possible you arrange things so that intentions are kept in the dark and events are treated as if they had not happened. It is not enough to confess that like anyone else, you too can have a weak moment. Whenever we meet any other person (a person who in the Christian sense is just as necessary as ourselves), we do so as people who are imperfect in some way and still need to learn. This fact must not only be admitted, it must be constantly confirmed in our actions as human beings. It is truly necessary to seek out this interaction with our fellows, no matter how much an occultist of the old school may dread it. It is not enough to simply protest against blind admiration; we must also seek out objective criticism.

In communities of this sort, spiritual teachers must renounce all the help available to them in pre-Christian times for making students receptive to their teachings. Above all, they must renounce the unapproachable authority of the teacher filled with divine wisdom, who taught students in whom the I had not yet been born. They must also do without the complete isolation of teachers and pupils from all human relationships. The problem I am pointing out here did not exist for pre-Christian initiators. The individual I had not yet been born, and the divine being working through the teachers had the authority to intervene in the destiny of the students in ways otherwise reserved for karma. But as Christians, we must see modern initiates first and foremost as human beings, and our confidence in them depends on them not exercising any superhuman influence on our destiny.

For someone who is directing all his energies toward the renewal of occult teachings for our times, the temptation is great to reject the difficult tasks of Christian community and to artificially make his teaching easier by any of the means appropriate in earlier times. However, these things have become evil in our times, and it would be better nowadays for the teacher to remain invisible except when promulgating the doctrine than it would be for him to relate to his students as you are doing. Maintaining and strengthening the I of each student is much more important than passing on the teachings—after all, the teachings are directed to the individual I. Any restriction of the ego's rights must also result in the teachings taking root within the individual in the wrong way. Any dulling of individual discernment represents a grave danger to those striving for the spirit.

I will admit that in one sense, this kind of right living is infinitely more difficult for you than for others. Christian occultists must take up a challenge that other people will face only in times to come; that is, to both live and be a seer. They are in constant danger of falsely confusing these different planes and the laws that govern them. But they cannot escape this danger by refusing the challenge; for without being able to orient themselves according to the Christ impulse, they would still get these two planes mixed up in unjustified ways. When this happens in a meeting with a pupil, the pupil will be the first to experience the disastrous results, although they will soon revert to the teacher.

The community of the Grail is perhaps the only place where this challenge has been met satisfactorily to any extent. You yourself admit that you are not totally satisfied with what you have been able to tell us about the Grail, and you have clearly described your own difficulties in researching the Grail mysteries, although you call the new initiates "initiates of the Grail." Perhaps the Grail will grant us salvation in this difficult hour.

Through the events I have described, my wife and I find ourselves in a situation with regard to yourself that makes it impossible for us to encounter you again in the way my wife did for the last time on Sunday, July 25, in the *Schreinerei*, and I on Thursday, August 5, on the steps leading to the eurythmy room. We were both in possession of this knowledge already at that time, as you were well aware. Nevertheless, you shook our hands and drew us into conversation as if nothing had happened. Healthy tact would have made that kind of thing impossible for any non-clairvoyant, so in your case I have to recognize it as an attempt at impermissible intervention into my inner being. I will refrain from explaining this statement in greater detail at this point because that would lead us too far afield.

It is still possible for me to greet you from a distance with all due respect as the bearer of great teachings, as I attempted to do on that evening. But I cannot submit to exchanging handshakes and friendly conversations with you as if nothing had happened, and especially not since I have clearly seen that these very handshakes and conversations are one of your chief means of exercising impermissible influences on your pupils and since I cannot share the opinion of a certain respected member that these things exist for the purpose of testing one's own strength in the face of outside influences.

To inform you of the need to avoid further personal contact is the purpose of this letter inasmuch as it concerns the two of us personally.

With regard to yourself, my purpose in writing to you about this very serious matter is to see accomplished the little I can do as your fellow human being, namely, to confront you with the fact that a person on the physical plane and using physical means has been able to point out to you the evil in your actions. You would be condemned to a shadowy existence if no one would turn to you like this. I hope that the fact that at least a few people nowadays are capable of recognizing your errors as such, remembering them and taking a stand against them, will be of help to you in the now necessary process of restructuring life in our spiritual movement. There are a few other members whom I can expect to understand the matters under discussion here, and I shall inform them of the contents of this letter.

It is imperative, however, that you begin to thoroughly transform the relationship between yourself and other members of the movement, as I have indicated. The objective purpose of my writing to you is to express this in the hopes that our movement will continue to work in accordance with the intentions of evolution. What would be the consequence if you were to reject this challenge? At least in certain instances, you have already forfeited an activity that must have been assigned to you by the masters of the white lodge—the personal instruction of individuals. For as I have already said, a profound mistrust in your treatment of individual human destinies is all too justified. I can also not imagine how an esoteric lesson could take place under the prevailing circumstances.

If you restricted yourself to disseminating ever more aspects of the teachings but let everything else continue as before, and if not enough members were able to work their way through to the necessary insights, the Society would degenerate into an exoteric association at best. There are already certain signs of this happening, alongside the tendencies to evil and to stupefaction. Either that or, if your followers become aware of their responsibility, they will have to bring about a complete separation between the teacher and what is taught, leaving you to discharge the duties of your holy office as a guilty and tormented Amfortas among hungry and sorrowful disciples.

I am now coming to the end of what I want to say at present. I have not been able to clothe these insights—which I achieved under the guidance of the Keeper of the Seal of the Society for Theosophical Art and Style, who is under the protection of Christian Rosenkreutz—in the ideal form I had envisioned. The obstacles were still too great for someone only recently released from your spell. But I have decided to send the letter anyway because the moment demands it.

When I wonder about the emotions with which you will receive this letter, the question of whether you will find your way to people with whom you can go through this experience and begin the necessary transformations weighs on me especially heavily. This is an area where, in this Christian age, the occultist as such is bound to fail and must be simply a human among humans, just as Christ Jesus had to experience things on Earth that he could not experience as a God. May you turn to this Spirit for help!

Heinrich Goesch
Gertrud Goesch

* * *

I have read you this letter, my friends, because it concerns each and every one of you just as much as it concerns me, and because it seems obvious to me that you must each decide for yourself to what extent you believe its claims correspond to actual practice within our Society. Otherwise people might think that I am afraid of this charge of contributing to the "stupefaction" of our members, and that I do not see you as sufficiently independent to leave it up to each one of you to judge the situation individually as you see fit.

However, you must realize that a letter like this cannot be seen in isolation; it is a symptom of what is going on in our Society. That is why I will take no part in discussing either this letter or anything that will need to be done as a result of it. It is clear that it must be left up to the members to decide what needs to be done and how to go about it, at least to begin with. In particular, I will refrain from saying anything about the passage claiming that promises have not been kept. If assessing this matter is left to individual discretion, each one of you will know how things stand, since each one of you must know what you have been promised and whether the promises were kept. However, I would expect and request the Society as such, or those members living in the neighborhood of the building in Dornach, to take a decided stand on this issue in the very near future.

I myself will not get involved in discussions on the matter at all. There are only a few things I want to tell you, and I ask you to take my remarks as what I have to say in connection with what I have just read, especially because it is obvious from other symptoms, not just from this letter, that many things I have said to members in lectures here in the course of the last few weeks and months have had no effect at all.

First of all, there is one thing I would like to emphasize. My friends, I cannot allow anyone to dictate how I conduct myself with members of the Society. It is up to me, and me alone, to decide how I find it necessary to relate to them. This is not to be taken as any kind of guideline for you; I am simply speaking for myself. I will not allow anyone to prescribe in any way how I should interact with members, inasmuch as this interaction has to do with the sins of omission I am supposed to have committed against them.

There is a very deep and weighty reason why this has to be the way it is. Not only this letter, but also many other things that have come up in the Society intermittently down through the years and with increasing frequency lately, show that many people simply do not make an effort to understand the kind of responsibility carried by someone communicating esoteric truths. It seems that many of our members don't want to try to understand what it sometimes takes to speak even a single sentence of that sort. With all the spiritual preparation it takes to give a lecture, it is simply not possible to sit with different little groups of members until two in the morning every night chatting about all kinds of useless and superfluous stuff. This fact is not sufficiently appreciated, nor are many other things that people seem to require of me and that then get counted as sins of omission. I need my time, and I need it in a totally different way than what people seem to want to understand. If I weren't using it the way I am, you would be hearing the same kind of stupid esoteric views from me that you can hear so much of in the rest of the world. So much for the sins of omission.

I also do not understand how the statement that my dealings with individual members and with groups of members are not Christian enough fits together with the complaint that I am exerting an undue influence over you by means of black magic whenever I take the liberty of shaking hands with one of you or involving you in conversation. I am certainly open to changing this practice if the Society will make its views on the subject known, because it is up to you, of course, whether you want to shake hands or get involved in a friendly conversation with me.

137

If this opinion becomes prevalent, it should be expressed, and then handshakes can, of course, be avoided in the future. For reasons I expressed earlier, I will not go into this any further, but there is still one thing I must mention because it is so very typical.

There is a passage in this letter that reads as follows: "Through the events I have described, my wife and I find ourselves in a situation with regard to yourself that makes it impossible for us to encounter you again in the way my wife did for the last time on Sunday, July 25, in the *Schreinerei*, and I on Thursday, August 5, on the steps leading to the eurythmy room. We were both in possession of this knowledge already at that time. Nevertheless, you shook our hands and drew us into conversation as if nothing had happened. Healthy tact would have made that kind of thing impossible for any non-clairvoyant, so in your case I have to recognize it as an attempt at impermissible intervention into my inner being." Let me just mention that on the Friday before Sunday the 25th, a member of our Society approached me with an inquiry from Mrs. Goesch with regard to her child, who had fallen down and gotten hurt somehow. I responded by saying that if she wished, I could take a look at what was wrong with the child. Shortly thereafter that person returned, bringing Mrs. Goesch and the child to me. On the following Sunday, here in the *Schreinerei*, I intervened in the inner being of Mrs. Goesch by shaking her hand and asking her how the child was doing.

My encounter with Mr. Goesch on the stairs leading up to the eurythmy room on Thursday, August 5, consisted of my responding to Mr. Goesch, who had asked me whether it was all right for the child (whom I had just seen standing down by the door) to take part in eurythmy exercises again, by saying that of course that was entirely up to the parents, since what the parents wanted was the only thing to consider in whether or not the child should come to eurythmy again. At that point, I also made the mistake of extending my hand to Mr. Goesch.

These are the two instances in which I intervened in someone else's inner being by means of black magic.

Let me still comment on one more passage from the end of this letter: "I am now coming to the end of what I want to say at present. I have not been able to clothe my insights—which I achieved through the guidance of the Keeper of the Seal of the Society for Theosophical Art and Style, who is under the protection of Christian Rosenkreutz—in the ideal form I had envisioned. The obstacles were still too great for someone only recently released from your spell." I believe you all know who the so-called keeper of the seal is, and all I have to say about this is that the person in question has written a number of letters to both me and my wife in the past few months, including one Mrs. Steiner received only today.[4] I will not discuss the matter of the "keeper of the seal" any further today; I just want to point out that her letters started coming around Christmas, mysteriously enough.

It may well be that I shall have to say something about this at some point, but I really do not want to do it today. I want you to come to a conclusion without being influenced by me. It is certainly almost impossible to be aware of the mysterious connection between this letter and the "keeper of the seal" and say nothing further about it, but today may not be the right time for that.

However, I do still want to mention that some years ago in fall I announced that due to certain embarrassing symptoms that had appeared within our Society, it seemed necessary to found a society of a more restricted sort.[5] To begin with, I attempted to invest a number of long-term members close to me with certain offices, on the assumption that these people would become independently active in accordance with their new titles. At that time, I said that if anything came of it, the membership would hear about it by Epiphany. No one heard a thing, which means that the Society for Theosophical Art and Style does not exist. That is a perfectly justified assumption, since no one has heard anything to the contrary, and it is equally safe to assume that an announcement would have been made if my intentions had in fact been realized. The way my plans were received, however, made it impossible for this society to come about. It was simply an experiment.

My friends, I have often said that the Anthroposophical Society has to make sense as a society if it is to make sense at all. After all, other arrangements could be made for lecturing on esoteric teachings. I have also often pointed out that if certain signs and symptoms continue to appear in the Society, finding another form for it will become inevitable because the present form and present arrangements are not serving the purpose. I was trying to avoid certain things prevalent in the Theosophical Society when I founded the Anthroposophical Society, of which I do not want to be a member, since that is crucial to what I have to do for this spiritual movement.

Our Society also often comes under attack from outside, and of course these attacks are also directed at the Society's teacher and lecturer. This should lead our active members to take up the obligation to defend our cause, if they take the idea of our Society as seriously as they should. However, libelous pamphlets of the most despicable sort, containing the most unbelievable calumnies, have been appearing, and I leave it up to each one of you to judge whether everyone who could do something about them has taken the idea of the Society as seriously as would be necessary if the Society is to withstand these attacks from outside.

My friends, it is neither feasible nor possible for those who have an interest in the survival of the Anthroposophical Society to always first come to me to discuss what they ought to do in defense of me and our cause. That has to come to an end. If it does not, it would mean that it is actually true that people here are assigned their positions by me. I have to respect the independence of the members, even if that means, as it unfortunately does in many cases, that I have to deny them something.

The fact of the matter is that the way things have been going, I could truly have done much more if I had not had to get involved in a lot of things that actually did not warrant my involvement. At least where the well-being of our Society is concerned, it is an absurdity to want to clear everything with me first. If what I want to do is to be accomplished on behalf of the Society, then please allow me the time to do it. The Society is wrongly conceived of if people are always turning to one individual; it must include taking personal initiative in what needs to be done on behalf of the Society.

For this reason, my friends, today's incident must be seen as an important and even crucial one. That is why I read you this letter, which is basically only an isolated symptom of something flaring up here, there, and everywhere. I will wait patiently to see what you, as members of the Society, will do about it. Meanwhile, I will continue to fulfill my obligations; the program will continue tomorrow as planned. But it goes without saying that how everything goes on after that will depend on the position the Society takes on what it has heard today. This is not something to be taken as an isolated case; it touches on many fundamental issues I have been pointing to for months in many discussions.[6]

* * *

When Rudolf Steiner had finished, a discussion took place; no stenographic record was kept. Some people must have spoken up in defense of the point of view expressed in Goesch's letter, because as one participant recollects, Rudolf Steiner left the room together with Marie Steiner, saying "I cannot have anything more to do with a society like this!"[7] The great majority of those present must have been ashamed of this state of affairs, and on that same evening they composed this expression of confidence:

141

Dornach
August 21, 1915

Dear Dr. Steiner:

As members of the Anthroposophical Society, we wish to express our righteous indignation and our feeling of shame that someone of mendacious and immoral outlook, as evident in Mr. Heinrich Goesch's letter, has dared to address you in a fashion dictated by the most despicable delusions of grandeur.

We must painfully reproach ourselves for not having understood how to prevent what has happened and for having proved unable thus far to create a circle of people in which the thoughts and feelings expressed in this letter could not have arisen.

We ask your forgiveness as our loved and respected teacher. We also ask that you not retract your confidence in us, or rather, that you trust in us again, because we are firmly resolved to better realize the ideal of the Anthroposophical Society and to be more aware of our responsibility in future.

It is a matter of course that, given the point of view they represent, we no longer wish to consider Miss Alice Sprengel, Mr. Heinrich Goesch, and Mrs. Gertrud Goesch as having a place in our midst.

We ask you, dear Dr. Steiner, to take our signatures as an assurance of our unconditional and constant trust and our sincerest gratitude.

signed by Michael Bauer and over 300 others[8]

* * *

This vote of confidence was a spontaneous and purely human expression of the signers' relationship to Rudolf Steiner. The facts of the case are addressed in Rudolf Steiner's own contributions. The professional comments of one Dr. Amann (Basel, September 14, 1915) shed some light on the difficulties the members faced in judging the situation:

Among the members, the prevailing opinion is still that Mr. Goesch is not mentally ill, he is only under a bad influence.

When someone has a fever or is drowsy, that is easy enough for anyone to diagnose. On the other hand, mental illness is extremely difficult for even an expert professional to diagnose except in extreme cases.

From people's comments, it is clear that they *cannot* understand that Mr. Goesch is mentally ill and that they have misconceptions about this type of illness. They believe the mentally ill are necessarily idiots who cannot write intelligently.

Idiots are feeble-minded; the sluggishness of their brain does not allow them to think at all. Unless some organic illness causes feeble-mindedness as a secondary condition, they are born retarded. Exactly the opposite is true of someone who is mentally ill; here, we are dealing with a melancholy frame of mind and clouded logic. This condition, in turn, must be distinguished from insanity—insane people are dangerous!

People who are mentally ill forfeit none of the quality of their intellect. Their intellectual capacity actually increases, because they are inexhaustible when it comes to intellectual work; in fact, they are intellectually active all day and all night. Their illness lies in the fact that they become obsessed and hypnotized with their own fixed trains of thought and are not susceptible to any criticism from outside. These people suffer in secret under the thoughts that plague them until they have carried them to term and can present them to the public. The urge to be visibly productive and important is constantly present in them.

Rudolf Steiner continued in the same vein on the following evening, August 22, 1915, discussing the case further.

III

Address by Rudolf Steiner

TODAY I would have liked to be able to lecture on a theme going beyond the events of the moment, and I hope that will be fully the case with tomorrow's lecture, which will begin at seven o'clock. For today, however, I still feel the need to say a few things that relate not only to the letter I had to read yesterday, but also to the very gracious letter from the members that Mr. Bauer has just delivered to me and to still another letter I have received. This is especially necessary now that the things discussed in these letters have come to pass. What I have to say will relate to the matter at hand only to the extent that this particular case can show us all kinds of things we need to know about the relationship of the details of what is going on among and around us to our spiritual movement with its teachings, for in discussing specific occurrences, it is often possible to discover something of universal importance.

I will start from the fact—speaking more or less aphoristically—that I read you a letter yesterday that was signed by two members of the Society and mentioned a third member of long standing.

I believe I will not be committing an indiscretion in telling you about a letter that Mr. Bauer showed me just fifteen minutes ago, a letter written by a Society member who is a physician.[1] The writer is quite rightly of the opinion, as I myself was yesterday, not only after but during the reading of Mr. Goesch's letter, that we are not dealing with anything logical but with something that has to be considered from the point of view of pathology.

Obviously, this is one of the many assumptions we can make in this instance, but in my opinion—and this is simply my personal opinion and should not be considered binding on anyone else—this assumption would be incomplete if we do not also ask whether we are allowed to tolerate the fact that our Society and our entire movement are constantly being endangered by all kinds of pathological cases. Are we to tolerate psychopaths who are destroying our spiritual-scientific activity? Yes, to the extent that we can have compassion for them. However, if we tolerate them without fully taking their pathological nature into account, we allow them to constantly endanger everything that is most precious and most important to us. Of course, we need to be clear that we are dealing with psychopaths, but we must also be clear about what we have to do so that our cause is not jeopardized. Even things we recognize as being caused by illness have to be dealt with appropriately in real life. Of course, how this applies to the personalities in question is a totally separate issue.

As you have seen from many things we have had to discuss over the course of time, there is a certain recurrent experience that is unavoidable in a spiritual movement such as ours: Personal interests and personal vanity inevitably get mixed up with our purely objective aspirations. This need not even be taken as a reproach, strictly speaking; after all, we are all human. But it does need to be mentioned, and I am simply stating my personal opinion on the subject; of course, you are not bound by my opinion. When people are willing to admit that they are subject to vanity in certain areas and that for the time being (perhaps for reasons having to do with their upbringing and so on) they have no particular interest in getting rid of that vanity, that is a much lesser evil than wanting to be absolutely perfect at any given moment. The greatest evil, so it seems, is when people want to believe in their own perfection in every instance, when they want to believe that they are doing whatever they are doing for totally selfless reasons, and so forth.

The greatest temptation faced by any spiritual movement such as ours is the very pronounced vanity that comes into play simply because such movements must necessarily have great and noble aims that can be realized only gradually, and not all of us can immediately broaden our interests to include the objective requirements of our cause. It is understandable enough that when some people first hear about reincarnation, they take an immediate personal interest in finding out about their own previous incarnations for reasons of personal vanity. Looking into history for this reason is the worst possible way to investigate previous incarnations, but that is what most people do out of personal vanity. Thus, instead of being an inner path of meditation, historical events or the Old and New Testaments become a treasure trove for the gratification of personal vanity. Simply put, it is nothing more than that. And it is good to be aware that looking for one's own incarnations in history or in the Bible is basically nothing more than personal vanity.

It is understandable that this kind of vanity should come into play. The trouble starts, however, when vanity is not recognized as such, and when instead of examining their deep-seated ambitious motives calmly, people shroud them in a mantle of occultism or let them merge into some nebulous mysticism.

Concerning certain things that prevail with some justification outside the confines of a spiritual movement, the movement must make a point of approaching them from the perspective of a much more elevated morality than is the norm. However, we must never disregard the possibility that a lot of what we consider higher morality may be nothing of the sort, but simply an outlet for our own drives and instincts. From the kinds of discussions we have been through before, you can see how people can have perfectly legitimate human instincts and drives, but let them get mixed up with all sorts of occult embellishments. They may even console themselves for the existence of these drives and instincts with all sorts of deceptively rational explanations. It would be much better if they would simply admit these drives exist and apply their esoteric schooling to understanding them.

I read Mr. Goesch's letter to you; you all heard it and followed what was going on. What I am going to say about it today is simply my personal, non-binding opinion. Among other things, it was stated in this letter: "I am now coming to the end of what I want to say at present. I have not been able to clothe these insights—which I achieved under the guidance of the Keeper of the Seal of the Society for Theosophical Art and Style...in the ideal form I had envisioned."

We all know that Miss Sprengel is the keeper of the seal and that Mr. Goesch is the one who wrote the letter. I think if any French-speaking people were to read this letter and apply the old French proverb "cherchez la femme," they would be quite right, in spite of the fact that "keeper of the seal" is a masculine noun in German. In fact, if you apply the principle of "cherchez la femme," much of what is talked about in this letter becomes more understandable.

I still need to express my own personal opinion about some of the details in this letter. For instance, in this letter it is suggested that it is impossible to imagine that so-called lessons of the esoteric school could be held within our Society after all that has happened. I read that passage yesterday. It suggests that because of all the "crimes" the letter describes, lessons of the esoteric school could no longer be held.

We must look at these things, too, in the right light and not hesitate to look at them closely. As you know, we temporarily discontinued these esoteric lessons when the war broke out, and anyone who bothers to look at these things carefully will realize that this is due to nothing other than the present circumstances of the war.[2] These lessons are not being given anymore so as not to do our Society a disservice.

There are only two possibilities these days. One is to act in the best interests of the Society, which means that regardless of whether we live in a nation at war or a neutral country, we must refrain from holding meetings that are not open to the public. Just imagine what could happen, and what a windfall it would be for people who go around making insinuations, if we were to hold secret meetings behind locked doors. Obviously, we must not do that, and Society members will have to resign themselves to doing without these lessons. It is as clear as day that we cannot have meetings between members from different countries going on behind locked doors, which is not to say that anything unacceptable would be happening there. As far as we are concerned, such meetings could happen on a daily basis as a matter of course. But you know how strong the opposition to our movement is. This must also be taken into account, and we must not endanger the whole movement by doing anything stupid or foolish. That's why we must give up holding closed meetings—they would simply open the door to that modern illness known as "spy-itis."

The other possibility, which is totally out of the question, would be to separate the members according to nationality in order to speak to them. That is obviously not in line with the purpose of our Society.

I hope you have realized by now that this measure was taken because the war made it necessary; it will be rescinded as soon as the war is over, as you could all have worked out for yourselves.

I must still mention a few more thoughts in connection with this measure. We cannot simply assume that all the people out there are so decent and respectable that they will assume that we, too, are only capable of decent and respectable actions. We cannot expect them to be concerned about us and about finding out what we are doing. They have no way of knowing whether or not we are doing something they would consider unacceptable. That is what stands behind taking measures like this. It is impossible to count on the outside world making positive assumptions about us, but we really ought to be able to count on this within the Society itself.

In recent months, not only in this letter but in all the events leading up to it, we have repeatedly heard the opinion—coming from people whose aspirations are expressed in this letter—that the lessons of the esoteric school have been stopped not because of the war but because the Society has assumed a form that makes it necessary for such lessons to stop altogether. After all, given the "crimes" that have been committed, it can no longer be assumed that people will have the requisite trust in such lessons. This means nothing less than that we have to expect that certain measures we take within the Society will be judged in a way that can no longer be considered a decent or respectable interpretation. This interpretation is absolutely inadmissible; it is real slander and cannot be excused as a simple mistake.

Legally speaking, it is no different from libel, and it is even more worrisome when the rumors being spread are veiled in all kinds of mystical disguises. The way such things are passed around is often much more disastrous than people imagine, although I wouldn't go so far as to endorse the point of view of this letter-writer and claim that rumors whispered from one person to another must necessarily make use of black magic. That is not what I mean. Spreading rumors can be accomplished by quite natural means and does not necessarily imply any talent for black magic.

Let me emphasize once again before I continue that what I am saying is my own opinion, not to be taken as binding on anyone else.

In the letter in question, there was much talk of how people are supposed to have been unduly influenced through me. I will not comment on the contradiction inherent in this—on the one hand, my friendly conversations and handshakes are interpreted as techniques of black magic, and on the other hand I am blamed for not seeking closer relationships with members. On the one hand it is stated that I cut myself off from the members and don't do enough for them, but on the other hand I am supposed to have used each and every conversation and handshake to influence people against their will.

We need to understand how such a contradiction can come about. For instance, someone may desire something—let's take the case of a person who wants to have been the Virgin Mary in a previous incarnation. This is a real example, not a made-up one. Suppose the person in question comes and makes me aware of this. If I were to say, "Yes, yes, my occult research confirms that," then that person would most likely not take this remark as an instance of undue influence. If what people are told corresponds to their desires, they are extremely unlikely to interpret it as an attempt to influence them unjustifiably. Now, self-deception and vanity are not usually taken to such an extreme that people imagine themselves having gone through this particular previous incarnation—they are more likely to choose something else, but the principle involved is what we need to consider at this point.

At this stage of human evolution, the autonomy of individual souls must be respected in the most painstaking way. Basically, people who think like the person who composed this letter do not have a viable idea of this painstaking kind of respect. After all, the writer of this letter would have found it pleasant to have been influenced in line with his own desires, and he wished for much more personal discussion. Suppose he and I had actually discussed all kinds of stuff, and also exchanged handshakes. On the one hand, that would have been exactly what he wanted, and on the other hand, the terrible crime he mentions would have been committed against him. As I said, most people have no idea of the painstaking regard for individual freedom that has to be the rule in a movement like ours. We must make an intense effort to preserve the autonomy of individual souls. Let's imagine people coming to us with relatively mild cases of incarnational vanity. If we agreed with them, they would surely not go on complaining about being unduly influenced. But suppose we said to them, "Don't be silly; never in all your previous lives were you any such person!" If we are being very precise about it, that would have to be considered an unjustified intervention in these people's inner being, although perhaps not a very serious one.

Let's look at this instance with all possible clarity. If people come to us and tell us who they think they were in an earlier incarnation, regardless of whether they have come to this conclusion out of vanity or out of something else, they have arrived at it themselves, out of their own individual souls. This is where their own soul's paths have led them. And it belongs to the fundamental nature of our movement to lead people further, if possible, starting from whatever point they have arrived at inwardly when they come to us, but not to break their heart and will at some particular moment. If in such a moment we simply make an end of the matter by saying, "Don't be ridiculous; that's nonsense," that is not an appropriate response. It actually would be an unjustified intervention if we permitted ourselves to speak like this, and these people would have no option but to extend us their confidence in a very personal way not appropriate to the situation, which, as we shall soon see, requires a totally different kind of confidence.

Instead, we should really say something along the lines of, "Well, as things stand now, this thought is something you have arrived at in your own soul. Try to make this thought carry over into real life; try to live as if it were true. See if you can actually do what you would be able to do, and if what happens is what would have to happen if it were true." An answer like this helps them arrive quite logically at how things really are. It truly preserves their personal freedom without cutting anything off

151

short, no matter how erroneous a path they may have been on until now. It is important to realize that refraining from influencing other souls is actually a very deep issue.

If they stick to the facts, people who share the opinions expressed in this letter will also not be able to maintain that any individuals in this Society have been particularly spoiled by me when it comes to having their previous incarnations made known. Please take what I have just said extremely seriously: It is not adequate to have some clumsy idea of what it means to influence or not influence others; in this day and age, if we always try to respect the freedom and dignity of others, the standards we must apply will be extremely difficult to live up to.

I have always consciously cultivated this sort of respect for the souls of others within our Society, to the extent that, in my attempt to preserve individual freedom, I have made a habit of speaking much less affirmatively or negatively than most people probably would. I have always tried to say only what would enable the person in question to come to independent conclusions on the matter, without acting on my authority. I have tried to eliminate personal authority as a factor by simply advising people to take certain things into account. This is something I have always made a conscious effort to foster.

I hope you will also realize that the misconceptions set down in this letter are not even among the strangest ones that can come about. It has happened more than once that people showed up at a lecture cycle somewhere or other, saying that it was Dr. Steiner's expressed wish that they attend. That has happened many times. If you look into it a bit, you will find that the people in question had told me of their plans to attend the series and, since I am always heartily pleased to meet members again in different places, I had told them I was very glad. In many cases, however, what I said was so changed in the minds of the people in question that by the next day they were saying that it was my particular wish that they attend this course. This is another instance of these strange misconceptions.

Many of our friends want nothing more than to be told what to do, but I have always tried to conduct myself so the members would notice that it would not occur to me to want to give people personal advice about how to manage their everyday life. I am far from wanting to influence them in things like whether or not they should attend a certain lecture cycle. From my perspective, the thing people most often want me to do and that I have to resist most strongly is to influence them personally in details like this. I never want to do that and always have to refuse. Within a society such as ours should be, it is necessary to refrain from that kind of thing.

All of this relates to something else that needs to be stated once just as a matter of principle. Anyone who observes how I try to work will realize that I always attempt to let the matter at hand speak for itself. And that brings me to the issue of confidence, as I would like to call it. I would really like to ask you members to duly consider whether I have ever done anything with regard to either an individual or the Society as a whole to encourage confidence of a personal nature in myself. Try to think about this and come to a conclusion on the basis of how I hold my lectures.

Let us consider an obvious case. You were all so kind as to show up for the lecture I held two days ago on various mathematical and geometrical ideas.[3] In the course of this lecture, I told you that from a certain spiritual scientific perspective, matter is nothing; matter as we know it is a hole in space. There is nothing there where matter is. However, I do not want you to simply take this statement on faith; I am far from wanting anyone to take these teachings on faith simply because they come from me. Instead, I try to show how modern science, including its most advanced and respected representatives, can arrive at the same insight as spiritual science. I tried to demonstrate an objective basis in fact, a basis that is also revealed by the results of scientific research, regardless of my own personal way of arriving at this discovery and quite apart from the fact that I am the one telling you about it.

I make a point of doing this so you will not need personal faith in me, but will be able to do without it and see how I try to let the subject, no matter how difficult, speak for itself.

I am sorry to have to present the issue of confidence to you like this; I would have preferred for you to see for yourself that all my efforts are directed toward making confidence in a particular personality unnecessary. The only kind of confidence that comes into question here at all would be the kind enabling you to say, "He is really making an effort to not simply lecture us on some kind of inspired insights; he is really trying to get everything together in one place so that things can be assessed on their own merit, independent of his personality." Of course, this is not to say that I always succeed in "getting everything together in one place"—first of all, there isn't enough time for that, and secondly it is the nature of things to remain incomplete. My method, however, does tend in the direction of eliminating rather than encouraging faith in me personally. That is how we have to look at this issue of confidence in a spiritual movement. That is what is important to me, but in this, too, I am only expressing my personal opinion.

Admittedly, we must also recognize a certain perspective that tends to make everything relative, since in general it is true that everything should be subject to legitimate criticism. And it is certainly true that everyone should have the right to criticize where criticism is justified. On the other hand, this business of criticizing must also be taken relatively. Just think, the amount of work we can do is limited by time and cannot be extended in just any direction according to the whims of others. In view of that, you will realize that some of Mr. Goesch's ideas have not been thought through in terms of real life.

As I have often pointed out and can state quite openly, I would not venture to speak about certain things if I had not lived and worked with them for decades and become familiar with them over the course of a long life. For example, I would never have spoken about *Faust* if I had not lived my way into it over decades of intense involvement with the subject.[4] Having done so, however, it is a real waste of time for me, as you can imagine, if someone who has not put anywhere near that kind of effort into it comes and wants to argue certain points with me. You really cannot ask that of me or of anyone else. Someone once wrote a letter to the poet Hamerling on the occasion of his fiftieth birthday, addressing him as "Dear old man"; Hamerling was somewhat taken aback, needless to say.[5] Now, I am over fifty already, but I think you will admit that my task demands a certain amount of time and will understand that I do not need to spend time debating with people about things I was already concerned with when those people were still in diapers. In the abstract, getting involved in such discussions may be the right thing to do, but it is not usually very fruitful, especially when it has to do with things like the contents of this letter. I really have to say that. It is quite a different thing when someone speaks out of age and experience than when some young upstart talks about it. That is simply a fact of life.

And then, just think about the blatant contradictions in this letter. You don't have to think as I do, but I do want to tell you what I think about it. One sentence reads: "Alongside the work dedicated to the good within your activity in our spiritual movement, I have noticed certain behaviors...," and so on. In conjunction with this sentence, the writer lists a large number of undertakings that I would not presume to mention myself if they weren't listed here, since I would have to admit that everything on this list has been done imperfectly at best. I have always emphasized, for instance, that the *Johannesbau* represents only the beginning of what ought to be done. Even so, people do not seem to be able to understand that I might have to limit what I take on, that I cannot, in addition to all these activities, take the time to cultivate all the relationships dreamed up by the writer of this letter. It is really taking things too lightly to imagine that I can possibly do both.

I am reluctant to put it like this, and I ask you to recognize my reluctance, but in order to do all that I would really have to ask the person who composed this letter to make each year twice as long. Barring that, I have to be permitted to organize my own activity as I see fit, which, however, in no way limits what other people want and can do. That, in fact, has been the goal of all my efforts—that each person should do what he or she wants without anyone asking them to do anything other than what they want to do. In that case, however, I must also be granted the right to limit what I recognize as my own task. In most cases, it is just those people who do not want to get involved in any concrete tasks and do not want to develop their will to serve concrete purposes who are most involved in criticizing what has already been accomplished.[6]

However, this is not a constructive attitude in real life. People who are not in agreement with an association as it already exists are welcome to stay out of it, and to do whatever they are in agreement with. It is much easier, though, to become part of some society and criticize it from within than to do something on your own initiative. Finding fault is easy, but it in no way determines or restricts what you yourself can accomplish. Knowing what ought to happen and that someone else is doing something badly is never the crucial factor, but what is crucial is the effort someone makes to actually carry out what one talks about and is able to do. It is also not crucial that other people carry out what I want to have happen—they can take it up or leave it; their freedom is limited, not by me, but only by what they believe themselves able to accomplish. They must simply develop the will to carry out what lies within their own capabilities.

When this Society of ours was in the beginning stages, I believed it could be a prime example of this last-stated principle. It is the greatest failing of this day and age that people always want a tremendous amount but do not actually manage to do anything. Well, that is understandable enough. You see, anyone who has acquired knowledge and capability in any particular field and works with what has been learned knows that what one can actually accomplish is really terribly little. People who have had to develop their abilities are the most aware of how little can actually be done, while those who can do very little or have not yet tested their abilities think they can accomplish the most. That is why programs are more visible nowadays than accomplished facts; programs are floating around all over the place. It is extremely easy to set down in abstract terms what we hope to achieve through socialism, theosophy, the women's movement, community with others, and so on. It's easy to develop ingenious and appropriate programs. But people who have done something positive, even within extremely limited circles, have actually accomplished much more than the ones who put out the greatest programs for all the world to see. My friends, we must realize that what counts is what actually gets done. It would be best if we would more or less keep our programs locked up in a secret chamber in our hearts and only use them as guidelines for our individual lives.

Of course, it is very easy to misunderstand a movement like ours. Yesterday, I pointed out that we have to accept misunderstanding as a matter of course and spoke about how we should relate to misunderstanding on the part of people outside the movement who are not only unsparing in their criticism—their criticism would actually be a good thing—but unsparing with slander and false accusations as well. A significant amount has been accomplished in this regard over the course of the years. Especially in the area of slander and disparagement much has been achieved; yet the steps necessary to fend them off have not been taken. It is really necessary that the most intimate attributes of a spiritual movement like ours spread within our Society.

Something I always advocate and repeatedly mention because it is obviously part of my task is the fact that what I can mean to another person must be determined only by the spiritual aspect of our movement. And it is crucial that this spiritual factor, this purely spiritual factor uniting us, not be misinterpreted. I really cannot discuss the issue of the case at hand without touching upon these things. I am very sorry about all this because I always try to protect people as long as possible. However, our cause has to be more important than individuals. There is no other way.

Anyone who can judge these things objectively will be readily able to see the connection between what I said earlier about respecting the freedom of each independent soul and how I relate to individual members. I am constantly trying to make a reality out of something that is a natural consequence of our spiritual movement and that seems necessary to me in order to handle all personal relationships in such a way that they are appropriately integrated into our spiritual movement. This means I must leave each and every member of our Society free to act in ways that may differ completely from mine.

Some of you may share Mr. Goesch's opinion, and welcome any efforts to cultivate our social and personal interaction and cohesiveness. I myself think it would be a good thing if someone would make this effort, so that our Society would be a society in more than name only. However, my own role in this Society is necessarily limited. Nevertheless, I realize that I am still the one who knows by far the greatest number of members personally. Many people here know fewer than I do. I am certainly not opposed to people doing a lot to cultivate the personal aspects that play such a great role in this letter, but as I said, I must limit what I myself take on for reasons I have already presented adequately.

In view of that, it seems a very strange misunderstanding of what is actually going on when we hear opinions like those expressed again in this letter, claiming that the best of what I have to offer is becoming a mere shadowy image because of all this. According to this point of view, it seems that this Society built on the basis of spiritual science, this Society as I have to understand it, is seen as something that is too abstract and ought to assume a much more personal character. I am putting it like this—"ought to assume a much more personal character"—in order to avoid using a different expression. I have often explained that this personal character is not possible; it simply cannot be. I have even said so to some members individually. I would prefer to see this personal element rooted out to such an extent that I could, for instance, lecture from behind a screen so as to avoid mixing up personal connections to members with the main point, which is to disseminate anthroposophical teachings and make them effective in actual practice. I am sorry to have to say things like this, but how are we supposed to understand each other if these things are not said?

I would like to relate a particular incident and then comment on it. There is a certain person to whom I have always related as I described above, trying to practice what is right in relation to our spiritual movement, fulfilling my obligations with regard to this movement and disregarding any personal factors.[7] Some time ago, this person found it necessary to write me a letter that begins as follows. I will not read the whole letter, but only the part of it that seems to be at the root of this whole incident. This letter arrived on December 25, 1914—Christmas Day of last year. I will now read this very characteristic passage, which begins with a quotation from one of the mystery dramas: "'Seven years now have passed,' Dr. Steiner, since you appeared to my inner vision and said to me, 'I am the one you have spent your life waiting for; I am the one for whom the powers of destiny intended you.'" Further on in the letter, we read, "Neither the teaching nor the teacher was enough to revive my soul; that could only be done by a human being capable of greater love than any other and thus capable of compensating for a greater lack of love."

This is asking for something that cannot and must not be given in a personal sense. The teacher and the teachings are of lesser importance; what is wanted is the human being, the person. We should not play hide-and-seek in cases like this. At the conclusion of Mr. Goesch's letter, he says that he arrived at his insights under the guidance of the keeper of the seal of the Society for Theosophical Art and Style. Now, this keeper of the seal is the same person who wrote the sentence I just read, a sentence that shows that the things she is writing about have been slowly coming to a head for a long time. I will refrain from using any adjectives to describe the particularly pronounced insinuations in the letter Mrs. Steiner received from her yesterday. (See p. 115.) Such insinuations should not be repeated because of course people should be protected as long as they actually allow themselves to be protected. However, I really must point out that it is possible for things like this to happen in our Society.

Please do not imagine that I have been blind to this development, which has split into two parts, so to speak. I will speak first about the part that has to do with our Society as it is seen from outside, since it may be best to talk about that aspect first. Among the many things, some of them highly slanderous, that have been written in defamatory articles about our movement in general and myself in particular, there have been ever-recurring insinuations about the number of man-chasing hysterical women in our Society. I am not saying that this is true, but simply that it is mentioned in the many diatribes that have appeared, slandering us and myself in particular.

The current case is not an isolated incident, and things that appear in this form should not be interpreted personally but taken as symptomatic. Still, I must say that someone trying to get close to our movement should not try to do so by writing "Seven years now have passed, Dr. Steiner..." and so on. I do not want to go into these things at great length, but you will understand what was meant. These things cannot be judged on the basis of a single case, however. Instead, each individual case has to be interpreted as a sign that the teachings have not been received as impersonally as they should have been, and as an indication that there were some among us ready to set less store by the teachings and the teacher than by the human personality.

This was one of the secondary reasons why I and my loyal colleague, who had stood by me for so many years, were married last Christmas. I admit that we were not at all inclined to conceal the matter behind any occult cloak. First of all, as far as we were concerned, these personal things were nobody else's business. Secondly, with regard to the relationship between us, it had become necessary not to let misunderstandings arise because of things being taken on a more personal human level than they were intended.[8] An expression used frequently between the two of us in those days was that by marrying me, Mrs. Steiner had become the "cleaning lady" with regard to things that had been accumulating in some people's heads. I think you understand what I mean. Our intent was to have things taken less personally than they had been until then.

I hope you will not misunderstand me when I say that in general in a society such as this one, liberating ourselves as much as possible from the customs of the rest of the world is not the point. Instead, we should be helping the world progress with regard to customs and ways of looking at things. It can only be of help to us to arrange such matters so they are quite clear in the eyes of the outer world and so no one can get mistaken ideas about them.

This also led Mrs. Steiner, in responding to a letter from the person who actually instigated this whole business, to write that a civil wedding ceremony was actually not such a terribly important event, considering our years of working together on things that were of utmost importance to our lives. The response to that was, "However, your civil marriage unleashed a disaster for me, one that I had feared and seen coming for years—not in what actually happened, you understand, but in its nature and severity." It should suffice for me to point out that a certain relationship exists between what we are experiencing now and the appointment of the "cleaning lady." As far

161

as I am concerned, no further proof of the need for the cleaning lady is needed!

There is no harm in taking things at face value and not reading more into them than is actually there, my friends, but it is always harmful to link a particular occult mission with some petty detail, or even something of major importance, from one's personal life. That's why we prefer the image of the "cleaning lady," which corresponds to the facts much better than any pompous pronouncements we might have come up with, although we never imagined we would have to talk about it.

It is my personal opinion that if someone in our spiritual movement looks for something so personal in things that are perfectly self-explanatory, it is a disturbing reminder of the prevalence of certain instincts in our Society. The only acceptable way to deal with these instincts is to admit that they exist and face up to them truthfully without any occult disguises. That is also the best way to move beyond them. It only works if you confront them for what they really are. In our circles, however, an incredible amount has been done to surround these things with an occult aura.

Why should we let the purely objective interest we actually ought to have in our spiritual movement be clouded by dragging personal vanity into everything? Why should we let that happen? People who spend a lot of time thinking about their incarnations down through history are not really interested in this cause; they lack the particular kind of interest they ought to have. The only difference between them and ordinary egotists is that ordinary egotists are not so presumptuous as to identify themselves with all kinds of historical incarnations, but satisfy their personal vanity with other things.

It is really true that it is much better for people to flaunt their clothes or their money than their incarnations—that is much the lesser of the two evils. These are things we have to take seriously and inscribe into the depths of our soul. They have done too much harm over the years and are so intimately bound up with what I am forced to call "personal vanity," to use a general term.

When personal vanity plays a large part, the most unbelievable misunderstandings can arise. As she recounts in her letter, this "keeper of the seal" once came to me and stated that she was obliged to apply standards already long since present within her to whatever came toward her from the outer world. My response was, "Why should that mean you can't be part of our spiritual movement? Of course you can apply your own standards," by which I only meant that our teachings have nothing to fear from anyone's personal standards. That is what people are supposed to apply. In my opinion, there was nothing wrong with her wanting to apply her own standards. But the way she interpreted this showed that what she actually meant was that she was already in possession of everything spiritual that could be given her; she had already seen it in visions and thus was already in possession of it.

Then this woman went on to ask whether in that case she could or should become a student of mine. I do not know why she asked that; the question is a contradiction in itself. Well, all I can say is that it was an undeniable fact that she wanted to join us in spite of everything, and there was no way to prevent her from doing it. However, her claiming to be already in possession of it all and condescending to work with this movement while insisting on applying her own standards reveal a kind of vanity that is looking for something other than our teachings. After all, she did not need the teachings if she had them already. People are so unbelievably unaware of this kind of vanity, and it plays such a very great role in a movement like ours.

This person assumed that what was being taught actually stemmed from her, no less. That is somewhat difficult to understand. She must have found some reason to believe that in something in Mrs. Steiner's letter of response to her,[9] something that led her to point more specifically to this mysterious source of our esoteric movement. That is how this strange state of affairs came about. My friends, it is no longer possible to play hide-and-seek for the sake of protecting individuals; it is time for us to go into these things. In the seal-keeper's answer to Mrs. Steiner, she says, "Three years ago, like a sick person seeking out a physician, I asked Dr. Steiner for a consultation. There was something very sad that I had to say during that interview, and I have had to say it frequently since then: Although I could follow his teachings, I could not understand anything of what affected me directly or of what happened to me. I must omit what brought me to the point of saying this, since I do not know how much you know about my background and biography." She says this because I once had to hear a conversation in which this was discussed. "I was not able to express my need, and Dr. Steiner made it clear that he did not want to hear about it." It's true that I did not want to hear about it, but I did respond. You cannot just avoid things like that by indicating that you do not want to hear about them. "The following summer, however, we were graced with the opportunity to perform *The Guardian of the Threshold*; in it a conversation takes place between Strader and Theodora, a conversation that reflected in the most delicate way the very thing that was oppressing me. Perhaps Dr. Steiner did not 'intend' anything of the sort"—intend is in quotation marks—"nevertheless, it is a fact. Perhaps it was meant as an attempt at healing." In the passage in question from the mystery drama, Strader says he owes everything to Theodora.

When people write things like this, especially in an attempt at a formal style, though its grandiloquence contributes nothing to its clarity, we really cannot assume that it deserves to be treated as a personal communication. There is a lot that could be seen as personal, and I have mentioned none of that; everything I have mentioned is intimately related to the whole character and nature of our movement. If people don't want these things to be mentioned in public, they should not write them down. When the kind of attitude expressed in this letter becomes predominant, it undermines everything I am trying to accomplish with every word I speak and with everything I have been doing for many years.

If we are to go on working together, you must not remain ignorant of what I think my position among you should be. If in fact we are to go on working together, it will have to be on the same basis as before. We must find a way to create a form for our spiritual movement that will be appropriate to the stage of evolution of people in our day and age. That cannot happen, however, if all kinds of personal things take the place of what should be achieved and understood on a spiritual level. It astounds me that in these difficult times, when our interest should be focused on the development of a major portion of humanity, someone should have so little interest in the events of the day as to drag such highly personal interests into our Society. A person who thinks it permissible to live in the illusion that something did not happen the way she dreamed it would, and has nothing better to do than cause a crisis on that account, is really cut off from the most profound aspect of our times.

This is how these highly personal matters start creeping into our Society. However, personal matters cannot be allowed to enter our movement, not in this form and not in any other. People whose chief interest is in their own person will only find a place in our Society to a very limited extent. Generally, people who wrap themselves in a mystical cloud also attempt to do the same to those around them. It would be inconsistent to imagine that you yourself are everything under the sun and not have the people around you be something special too, so the tendency is to broaden the circle. But when, as so frequently happens, this purely personal interest and personal feeling of vanity take the place of objective observation of and efforts toward what our spiritual movement is meant to be, they inflict the worst possible damage on our Society.

One might have thought that the *Johannesbau* going up here would have presented enough problems to keep our members

165

busy and distract them from the vainer and more foolish things in life. One really might have believed that this building would turn their thoughts to better things. But as you see, that has not come about as we might have hoped, and yet we have to go on working. I thank you all for the expressions of confidence contained in the letter our friend Mr. Bauer brought to me, as well as those expressed by other members, and I hope ways and means can be found to deal with these obstacles to our movement's true progress and to give a little thought to what it will take to keep our movement from being too seriously constrained by outer hindrances in the future.

Criticism, my friends, cannot harm us. People can criticize us objectively as much as they like, and it will do no damage. First of all, it will always be possible to counter the criticism with whatever needs to be said, and secondly, time is on our side. Today, people may well still think we're fools because of our boiler house or the *Johannesbau* itself, or whatever, but they'll come around, and we can wait until they do. That's the way it is with anything new.

It is something totally different when slanderous and untrue statements are made. In that case, we are obliged to set these claims straight again and again if we don't choose to simply ignore them, and of course the slanderers can always answer back. It can even reach the point of taking legal action. Yet, we do need to defend ourselves against such statements, even if it feels like washing our hands in black and filthy water.

If we could really foster an active attitude and strengthen our forces on these two fronts, we would be able to do a lot that has been left undone so far.

Of course, this is not meant as a personal reproach to anyone in particular; some of what I said applies to some people, other things to others. It is intended quite generally. However, what I have pointed out has a solid basis in fact, and in order for you to see it, I have had to present something of the situation to show how things that were only intended to be taken spiritually have been taken very personally.

Please don't take it amiss if I say that if someone comes with complaints, even if she says she already knew everything she has gained or can still gain through the movement, the only thing to do is treat that person like a child and offer fatherly admonition or friendly consolation. I was naive enough to believe that it had helped, and then had to watch these delusions of grandeur appear afterward, so it...[*gap in stenographic record*] great damage within this Society of ours.

Considering the claims of the keeper of the seal, there was never any point in doing anything other than smilingly forgiving her for this rubbish, the way you excuse a child. Please don't hold it against me that I said what simply had to be said. But for the sake of our movement's dignity, we cannot permit pathological elements to destroy it. That is why we cannot always take the stand that we should simply accept these pathological elements for what they are. When this pathological element takes on all the appearances of delusions of grandeur, we have to call it by name; we have no other choice. This is by no means directed against the personality in question, but only against what is deserving of criticism in that person. After all, we must face the facts and not hide the issue behind the cloak of the occult. It requires a particular effort at self-education to do that, but if we succeed, we will see things as they truly are instead of through a glass darkly.

Perhaps you will say that I myself am speaking out of vanity at this point. That will make no difference to me, since I have already been condemned to call a spade a spade in this instance. I have known many students who thought they were smarter than their teachers and proceeded to tell them off, claiming that the latter had made all kinds of promises without keeping them. That this should also happen within our Society comes as no great surprise.

Now I have given you my own humble opinion, which you are not to take as binding. I am simply asking that you take it in the same way I want you to take everything I say, that is, I would like you to try to see if we are better able to get on with life in our movement once a common resolve is there to call the big things big and the little things little instead of drawing a mystical halo around any old arbitrary personal vanity.

If we are not aware of the full seriousness of our movement, the temptation is very great to fake it by decking out all sorts of life's little vanities in this same serious garb. That cannot be, and this simple statement means more than it seems to. This is what I had to say, although I did not want to. I cannot read these letters in their entirety in front of the whole movement, but it would not occur to anyone who could read them that I have overstepped my authority by quoting passages from private correspondence. In this case, it had to happen because these things are related to the very foundations of what we are doing together.

IV

Resolving the Case

IN MEETINGS on August 25 and 26, 1915, between the *Vorstand* and the members of the Society, meetings Rudolf and Marie Steiner did not attend, the decision was made to no longer recognize Heinrich and Gertrud Goesch and Alice Sprengel as members of the Society. As a result of these meetings, the following resolution was sent to Marie Steiner:

Dornach
August 27, 1915

Dear Madam:

The *Vorstand* has presented you with the unanimous request of the assembled members that you be so kind as to retain the office you currently hold within the Anthroposophical Society.

As members, we wish to heartily confirm this oral communication with our signatures.

With deepest respect and thanks for the blessings bestowed on the Society through your work, we are

Devotedly yours,

(ca. 300 signatures)

* * *

The series of seven lectures included in this volume on the conditions necessary for the survival of the Anthroposophical Society began on September 10. On September 11, on the basis of discussions among members that had taken place in the meantime—discussions in which Rudolf and Marie Steiner had not taken part—a meeting of the *Vorstand* was held. It was decided to produce a thorough documentation of the Goesch/ Sprengel case for the membership and to postpone the implementation of their expulsion until this document had been completed. On the next day (September 12), a members' meeting was held in place of a General Assembly, since members from other countries were unable to attend due to the war. No transcript exists of this meeting, which was intended to confirm the resolutions of the *Vorstand*; from the few brief notes available, it seems that Rudolf Steiner did take part in this meeting.

In the course of the days that followed, the document that had been resolved upon was written up; it ran to twenty typed pages. It recounted explicitly the contents of the letter from Heinrich and Gertrud Goesch and included character descriptions of the three people in question as well as a statement that Rudolf and Marie Steiner had not been involved in the decision to expel them from the Society. All significant portions of this document have been taken into account in preparing the documentation included in this volume; in some cases the present reproduction of relevant documents is more complete. It is to be assumed, although it has not been proved, that this document was enclosed with the following letter sent to Heinrich and Gertrud Goesch and Alice Sprengel by the *Vorstand* of the Anthroposophical Society on September 23:

Due to the fact that you have taken a position that does not lie within the goals and premises of the Anthroposophical Society, the *Vorstand* of said Society is compelled to revoke your membership.

Michael Bauer
for the *Vorstand*
of the Anthroposophical Society
Dornach, September 23, 1915

* * *

On the following day, September 24, 1915, the women's meeting that had been proposed on September 17 took place. Its purpose was to talk about the position of women in ancient and modern esoteric movements, on the basis of what Rudolf Steiner had presented in his lecture on September 15. Marie Steiner had been asked to chair the meeting. According to handwritten notes she supplied, she spoke as follows:

Address at the Women's Meeting
Dornach, September 24, 1915

A number of female members who proposed today's meeting asked me to take the chair. In spite of the fact that I have scarcely had time to collect myself in the past few weeks, I will be glad to fill this role if that is also the wish of the rest of those present.

Not many written contributions were received beforehand. We will go through them in the order in which they were received. I will begin by reading the proposal that led to our gathering today, and will then say a few words.

[Reads the proposal to call this women's meeting]

The basic thought expressed in this proposal is the one that occupies me the most, too: We are a number of women who have been granted something that has been denied the female sex until now, something that shall serve to regenerate human-kind—its loftiest spiritual possession. How can we show our-selves to be worthy of it? It is a good thing to take this opportu-nity to be together to look at the full seriousness of our situation and our task, and to look at where we stand within the women's movement in general.

Out there, women are fighting for equal rights, for the oppor-tunity for free development alongside men. This struggle has been fraught with untold difficulties, and many of us once ex-hausted our best energies in it, some of us doing battle with mounting material obstacles, others unable to free themselves before collapsing under the weight of conventions and preju-dices and the tyranny of traditional attitudes.

All of a sudden, in the midst of this struggle, when it seemed that only certain individuals or future generations would be able to reap the fruits of all our exertions in the present, a door opened into the light and we were given a field of activity that surpassed all our expectations. It pointed out the way to our true goals, raising us up above the level of the unavoidable aberrations of a decadent and stagnating culture whose time is past. Now we could escape the danger of drowning in our de-sire to imitate, "monkey see, monkey do," what was going on in this male culture, paying the price of our eternally feminine soul and spirit in our running after outer cultural forms shaped by men.

We had been able to contribute to the stimulation and inspira-tion of this culture simply by virtue of the fact that we were not its servants, its executive organs. Turned back on ourselves, left to our own devices, we could develop attributes of inwardness, depth, warmth, softness, and reserve that were a necessary

172

counterbalance to what the men were having to achieve. We could tame, enthuse, comfort, support, heal, carry, sustain, and enliven within and without—no small task, to be sure. The men, meanwhile, were conquering the outer world.

Now they had conquered it; it was theirs. They measured its breadths, dissected its parts, became its master. Their intelligence was their downfall. Laughing in scorn, they shoved aside the old gods and the sources of their strength.

Then we, too, began to take notice, because the ground under our feet was beginning to shake. The old gods dead? Outer life the only thing that mattered? Our soul's vital wellspring, which had allowed us to feel instinctively the symbolic nature of all transitory life, mere illusion? Then let us out, too! Then we too must be allowed to break the bonds, to understand and work out of our own initiative and our own conviction. Let us, too, measure ourselves against the standards of this outer world! The life in us demanded its due, and we stormed onto the battlefield.

Two things we met there. On the one hand, the hard, immobile forms created by men. To conquer them, we had to subject ourselves to an iron discipline. Some of us succeeded. Not all of us were satisfied with that.

The second thing we found was outward freedom. There we stood, young and breathing deeply, in the breaking waves of life, the old oppressive chains far behind us. We had to discover our own standards, our own incorruptible guidelines, within ourselves.

Not all of us were able to do that. Many women felt as if they had been caught up in a whirlwind, and the untamed aspect of their nature broke through. Study, hard work, and the dry routine of professional life did not suffice for long; many in the droves of women that followed found them a burden. Freedom to express ourselves, freedom of experience were what we demanded—equal rights with men when it came to the pleasures of life, too.

The wave of materialism crested and broke and swept us women away with it. As our secure sense of the reality of a spiritual world died away, our instinctive life broke through with elemental force, distorted by the aberrations of our intelligence.

The theories of a Laura Marholm[1] were adhered to by the extremists of a group of female poets represented by people like Marie Madeleine[2], Dolorosa[3], Margarete Beutler[4], and so on. I am sure every country on the European continent experienced a similar phenomenon.

Literature offered proof that even the wildest erotic fantasies of men failed to unearth such excesses as we witnessed in the products of women's overheated imaginations. We shuddered to watch as women like these, driven by vanity and thirsting for glory, but poor in spirit and in knowledge, forced the products of their goaded sensuality into the long-since fixed forms of our language. They declaimed the results themselves in literary clubs; the men they had asked to do so on their behalf had responded that they would be ashamed.

The outlook was dim—desiccation and desolation on one hand, brutalization and licentiousness on the other. Where was the redeemer who would speak the word of life to help humanity on its further way?

Then a wonderful thing happened: In this age of decadent culture, moral decline, dulled thinking, and crass egotism, teachings appeared from seclusion, teachings that could formerly only be given to a few but could now become the common property of all humankind, teachings that would help humanity find its way out of spiritual desolation into the experience of the spirit. And women were allowed to take part in this work; here, if they so chose and if they made themselves worthy of it, was their new field of activity.

They approached this with a natural inclination toward the ideal, a greater mobility of thinking, and thus a high degree of receptivity. What they were lacking was discipline in thinking, the exactitude and precision, certainty of knowledge and the respect for this certainty, and the sense of reality that men in their professional activity had been forced to maintain. To put it crudely, their weaknesses were gossip, vanity, wishy-washiness, and the tendency to drag everything down to a sentimental and personal level. Their strong points were enthusiasm and readiness to make sacrifices. If women proved able to outgrow their natural level of existence as members of their species, these last two attributes would allow them to breathe life into a rigidifying culture. If they proved able to forget the personal aspects and become objective, they would be able to help build the future and be the equals of men in terms of rights, responsibilities, and significance in the new culture coming about.

Have we been able to meet these two conditions? Has our personal nature, our natural species-nature, stepped back into second place and become objective? I fear we have failed, on the whole.

Only when we bring our failings into the realm of consciousness and develop the will to understand, only then will we be able to overcome these failings and transform destructive forces into productive ones.

The task before us, the field of activity that lies open to us, is greater than any our most far-reaching wishes anticipated. But we cannot allow ourselves to lose the ground under our feet. We must not simply go into raptures, we must understand and work. For the first time since esoteric knowledge was granted to humankind, we women are allowed to receive this knowledge together with men and inaugurate a new era through this work in common.

Let me repeat, however, that in order for this new era in the history of humankind to reach its full potential, women will have to surmount their narrowly personal nature and the level of existence natural to our species. We must keep our spirituality pure and untouched by our desires, drives, and unclean thoughts.

It has been frightening to see that we are not necessarily able to do this. We women have been constantly mixing lower things in with the higher and cloaking sensuality with spirituality to make it seem like something it is not. Again and again, the three evil forces of vanity, eroticism, and falsehood have appeared in intimate connection with each other.

The reason for us being here is that these things have happened among us; we must try to confront our failings head on. We are faced with the question of whether we will be found to be unfit and unready. Will we throw away our chance at what could reenliven humanity?

What will we do if we are granted a grace period, time to think things over? What can we do so that men and women can work together free of distraction?

These are the questions we have to ask ourselves. Each one of us should contribute to answering them.

* * *

In response to the position taken by the *Vorstand*, expressions of confidence in Rudolf and Marie Steiner flowed in from many branches of the Society in the time that followed. Even Heinrich Goesch's brothers Paul and Fritz and Fritz's wife, all three of whom were members of the Society, dissociated themselves from their brother's actions. In September 1915, Paul Goesch signed a resolution of the members of the Berlin branch of the Anthroposophical Society expressing their "most profound disapproval of and pained indignation at the unheard-of behavior of Mr. and Mrs. Goesch."

How far Rudolf and Marie Steiner stood above this case is demonstrated by the fact that Marie Steiner still made it possible for Alice Sprengel to receive financial assistance after being expelled from the Society and leaving Dornach, as proven by this letter to a Miss Julia Wernicke, who had maintained contact with Miss Sprengel:[5]

Dornach
September 29, 1915

Dear Miss Wernicke:

Miss Waller showed me a letter she had received from you in which it was requested that she act on behalf of Miss Sprengel in collecting the money several members allegedly still owe her.[6] Since you yourself had to assume that not many people would be interested in this situation, which Miss Sprengel brought upon herself through her own excesses, and since Miss Waller has declared that she wants nothing to do with it, ordinary human compassion forces me to assume responsibility for the payment of this debt. I must ask that you not mention my name, however: first of all, that would be unpleasant for Miss Sprengel, and second of all I do not want to encourage any rumors about my having tried to accommodate Miss Sprengel in any way.

Acting on the basis of a letter from Mrs. von Strauss, I take the liberty of covering her debt.[7] When you send the money to Miss Sprengel, please tell her it is to cover that debt, but that you are not in a position to reveal names.

Yours faithfully,

Marie Steiner

* * *

With that, the 1915 case was brought to a temporary close. Although his relationship with Alice Sprengel ended shortly thereafter, Heinrich Goesch remained an unfair adversary, spreading spiteful untruths wherever he could. As late as 1923, he appeared in public in Berlin as a "non-anthroposophical expert on anthroposophy" and again spoke out against Rudolf Steiner. This will be documented in the volume on the history of the Society covering the year 1923.

177

Notes

ABOUT THIS EDITION

ABOUT THE TEXT: Several participants took notes during these lectures. Franz Seiler of Berlin was the official stenographer, but Helene Finckh of Dornach also recorded the entire series in shorthand. Summaries in shorthand were made by Bertha Reebstein-Lehmann and Johanna Arnold; in longhand, by Louise Boesé, and Elisabeth Vreede made a summary of three lectures.

All of these sources were taken into account in preparing this edition; the text was then compared to the original shorthand versions available. It is apparent from Seiler's transcription of the shorthand record that Rudolf Steiner himself read it through once and made some corrections, which were of course included in this edition. Apparently he intended to have the lectures printed for the information of the members. It seems that the editing became too time-consuming for him, however, because defects of greater or lesser magnitude remain in the text, which made it necessary to edit the lectures considerably before they could be printed. This editing, however, does not touch on Rudolf Steiner's train of thought.

ABOUT THE DRAWINGS: The drawings correspond to how the notetakers reproduced them. Seiler's version of the lecture of September 14, 1915, includes two of Rudolf Steiner's original drawings, which have been reproduced here in facsimile.

PUBLICATION IN JOURNALS: The lectures given in Dornach on September 10, 11, 12, 14, and 15, 1915, appeared in *What Is Happening in the Anthroposophical Society—News for Members*, Vol.16 (1939), nos. 2–13.

The title of this volume and the titles of individual lectures are the responsibility of the publisher.

PART ONE

In these notes works by Rudolf Steiner are referred to by their volume number in the Collected Works (*Gesamtausgabe* = GA). Translations of quotations in the notes are by the translator of this volume except when otherwise noted. Notes by the translator are in square brackets.

Lecture One
REQUIREMENTS OF OUR LIFE TOGETHER
IN THE ANTHROPOSOPHICAL SOCIETY

[1] In Stuttgart on September 4, 1921, at the first Members' Assembly after World War I, Rudolf Steiner addressed the question of the lecture cycles as follows: "Actually, every member has taken on the responsibility of seeing that the cycles stay within the Society. I am not so concerned about the cycles being read outside the Society; what matters to me is that these cycles in the form in which they were printed stay among people who understand the circumstances, because lack of time kept me from correcting the proofs." (*Mitteilungen des Zentralvorstandes der Anthroposophischen Gesellschaft*, Stuttgart, November 1921, No. 1, p. 27). And in *The Course of My Life*, GA 28, (Hudson, NY: Anthroposophic Press, 1986): "I would have preferred it if the spoken word could have been left in that form, the members wanted to have the lectures printed privately, and that is why the talks now exist in print. If I had had time to make corrections, there would have been no need for the 'for members only' restriction right from the beginning." (Chapter XXXV, Anthroposophic Press, 1986).

However, since the members did not feel bound by this responsibility and Steiner's opponents in their writings often showed themselves to be better informed about the lecture cycles than the members themselves, Rudolf Steiner was obliged to lift all restrictions and declare the printed lecture cycles available to the general public at the Christmas Foundation Meeting of the Anthroposophical Society in 1923.

[2] See the explanations Steiner gave on August 21 and 22, 1915, printed in Part Two of this volume.

[3] August 22, 1915, in Part Two of this volume, p. 144.

[4] "The Origin of Evil in the Light of Spiritual Science," Munich, March 29, 1914. Only incomplete notes of this lecture are extant.

5 Gustav Gräser, 1879–1958, who became well known as an apostle of nature in the 1920s. Cf. Ulrich Linse, *Barfüssige Propheten. Erlöser der zwanziger Jahre*, Berlin, 1983. ("Barefoot Prophets: Redeemers of the Twenties") Rudolf Steiner mentioned Gräser in a letter to Marie von Sivers on January 6, 1906 (in Rudolf Steiner/Marie Steiner-von Sivers, *Correspondence and Documents 1901-1925*, GA 262, (London: Rudolf Steiner Press, 1988), saying that Gräser had attended a lecture of Rudolf Steiner's and taken part in the discussion afterward.

Lecture Two
THE ANTHROPOSOPHICAL SOCIETY AS A LIVING BEING

1 Cf. Diogenes Laertius, *The Life and Opinions of Famous Philosophers*, VI, 40 (about Diogenes of Sinope): "When Plato proposed the definition, which met with approval, that the human being is a featherless two-footed creature, he (Diogenes) plucked the feathers from a chicken and brought it into Plato's school, saying, 'Here is Plato's human being.'"

2 August Weismann, 1834–1914, professor of zoology. Studies on the theory of evolution, 1875/6; lectures on the theory of evolution, 1881. Cf. Rudolf Steiner's lecture of April 18, 1916, in *Gegenwärtiges und Vergangenes im Menschengeiste* ("Things Past and Present in the Human Spirit"), GA 167, (Dornach, Switzerland: Rudolf Steiner Verlag, 1962).

3 The three points in the 1913 "Draft of the Principles for an Anthroposophical Society":

1. Within the Society, all those people may work together in a brotherly fashion who take as their foundation for lovingly working together the existence of a common spirituality in all human souls, regardless of their differences with respect to faith, nation, class, gender, etc.

2. Investigation into the supersensible concealed in everything sense-perceptible shall be fostered and the dissemination of true spiritual science promoted.

3. Knowledge of the core of truth in the philosophies of different peoples and times shall be fostered. [This draft was not published in English—Translator]

4 "What Are the Intentions of Spiritual Science? A Response to 'What Do the Theosophists Want'" in the *Tagblatt ("Daily News") für das Birseck, Birsig, und Leimental*, Arlesheim, Vol.43 no. 50, February 28, 1914. Now printed in *Philosophie und Anthroposophie. Gesammelte*

Aufsätze 1904–1923, GA 35, (Dornach, Switzerland: Rudolf Steiner Verlag, 1984). [See next note. Not published in English—Translator]

5 "What Do the Theosophists Want?"—a talk given at the family night of the Reformed Church in Arlesheim on February 14, 1914, by E. Riggenbach, pastor. It was printed in the supplement to the *Tagblatt*, Arlesheim, February 1914.

6 It has been reported that this is how the Italian Princess D'Antuni, Elika del Drago, expressed herself to Rudolf Steiner. At her invitation, Steiner held lectures in the Palazzo del Drago in Rome in 1909 and 1910. He used this expression quite a few times.

7 On March 5, 1616, under Pope Paul V and as a result of the turmoil surrounding Galileo, Copernicus's work, "De revolutionibus orbium coelestium libri VI" (1543) was placed on the Index of forbidden books by the Inquisition charged with that task. On May 10, 1757, the Index Commission resolved to rescind the decree forbidding books saying that the sun stands still while the earth moves in the new edition of the Index, and Copernicus's book was no longer listed in the Index from then on. However, it was only on September 11 and 25, 1822, that the Holy Office and Pope Pius VII allowed the printing and publication of such works.

8 See Part Two, pp. 123–135.

9 Dr. Hugo Vollrath, theosophical book dealer and publisher (Theosophisches Verlagshaus) in Leipzig. In addition to being a member of the German Section of the Theosophical Society led by Rudolf Steiner, he also belonged to the so-called Leipzig Society and tried to bring its intentions, which were quite different in their orientation, into the German Section. This made their cooperation very difficult. Primarily at the insistence of the Leipzig branch of the German Section, he was excluded from membership in the German Section by its VIIth General Assembly in October, 1908.

10 Rudolf Steiner, *Theosophy: An Introduction to the Knowledge of the World and the Destination of Man*, GA 9, repr., (Hudson, NY: Anthroposophic Press, 1988).

11 See Part Two, p. 170.

12 Several lines have been omitted here because the stenographic record did not make sense.

Lecture Three
SWEDENBORG: AN EXAMPLE OF DIFFICULTIES
IN ENTERING SPIRITUAL WORLDS

[1] Emanuel Swedenborg, b. Stockholm 1688, d. London 1722, scientific investigator, physician, and mystic.

[2] The *Autographa* edition, published by the Swedish Academy of Science, 18 volumes, Stockholm, 1901–1916.

[3] Presumably Rudolf Steiner is referring to the section on the planet Mars in Swedenborg's book *Die Erdkörper im Weltall* ("The Heavenly Bodies in Space"). Steiner had in his personal library the book *Emanuel Swedenborgs Leben & Lehre. Eine Sammlung authentischer Urkunden über Swedenborgs Persönlichkeit, und ein Inbegriff seiner Theologie in wörtlichen Auszügen aus seinen Schriften*, Frankfurt, 1880 ("Emanuel Swedenborg's Life and Teachings: A Collection of Authentic Documents on Swedenborg's Personality, and a Sample of his Theology in Verbatim Extracts from his Works"). (Publisher not given).

[4] Rudolf Steiner, *Chance, Providence and Necessity*, GA 163, (Hudson, NY: Anthroposophic Press, 1988).

[5] "The Path of Knowledge," *Theosophy*, pp. 154–178. See Lecture Two, note 10.

[6] In many lectures by Steiner, in addition to sections in the following books: *Theosophy*. (See Lecture Two, note 10.) *Knowledge of the Higher Worlds and Its Attainment*, GA 10, repr., (Hudson, NY: Anthroposophic Press, 1986). *An Outline of Occult Science*, GA 13, repr., (Hudson, NY: Anthroposophic Press, 1989).

[7] *Genesis*, GA 122, revised translation (London: Rudolf Steiner Press, 1982).

[8] In a lecture given on August 8, 1915, entitled "The Tree of Life and the Tree of Knowledge," not published in English but available in manuscript from Rudolf Steiner Library, Ghent, N.Y. 12075. Published in German in *Kunst- und Lebensfragen im Lichte der Geisteswissenschaft* ("Questions of Art and Life in Light of Spiritual Science"), GA 162, (Dornach, Switzerland: Rudolf Steiner Verlag, 1985).

NOTES

Lecture Four
METHODS AND RATIONALE
OF FREUDIAN PSYCHOANALYSIS

[1] Sigmund Freud, 1856–1939. Psychiatrist, founder of psychoanalysis.

[2] Joseph Breuer, 1842–1925. Rudolf Steiner met Breuer in the home of the Specht family, where Steiner was a tutor from 1884–1890. See Steiner's *The Course of My Life*, GA 28, Chapter XIII, (Hudson, NY: Anthroposophic Press, 1986). See also Karl König, "Die Schicksale Sigmund Freuds und Joseph Breuers" ("The Destiny of Sigmund Freud and Joseph Breuer"), Stuttgart 1962.

[3] In Joseph Breuer's therapy, hysteric patients were put under hypnosis and their symptoms traced back to the point when they first appeared; as a rule, on recreating this condition, the symptoms intensified, but usually disappeared afterward. In their *Studies on Hysteria*, (Leipzig and Vienna, 1895) Breuer and Freud described this form of therapy on the basis of five individual cases.

[4] Berlin, November 4, 1910, included in *The Wisdom of Man, of the Soul, and of the Spirit*, GA 115, (New York: Anthroposophic Press, 1971). Also Munich, November 18, 1911, in *Esoteric Christianity and the Mission of Christian Rosenkreutz*, GA 130, 2nd ed., rev., (London: Rudolf Steiner Press, 1984).

[5] Sigmund Freud, *Totem and Taboo*, tr. James Strachey, copyright 1950 by Routledge & Kegan Paul Ltd. (New York and London: W. W. Norton & Company). In the magazine *Imago*, vols. I and II (1912 and 1913), these articles appeared under the title, "Some Correspondences in the Inner Life of Savages and Neurotics."

[6] Dr. Oskar Schmiedel, 1887–1959, a chemist, was head of the laboratory producing the plant pigments needed in building the first Goetheanum.

[7] Freud, op.cit., p. 29.

[8] Ibid., p. 30.

[9] Apparently, the next few lines dealt with the connection between the Goesch-Sprengel case and psychoanalysis, but the stenographer only caught the words, "It is important how the connection is drawn ... with disguised drives like these ... especially between two personalities of this sort...."

[10] Sigmund Freud dealt with the Oedipus complex for the first time in *The Interpretation of Dreams*, tr. James Strachey, Chapter V, Section D, (New York: Avon, 1965).

[11] Freud, *Totem and Taboo*, p. 16.

[12] Ibid., p. 17.

[13] Moritz Benedikt, 1835–1920, physician and criminal anthropologist. The exact quotation reads, "Nowadays we find that students at the best finishing schools are more informed on the topic of sexual perversions than we young doctors used to be, and I often wish beating could be instituted as a punishment for the 'liberated' women teachers who encourage this kind of knowledge." *Aus Meinem Leben. Erinnerungen und Erörterungen*, Vienna, 1906, vol. II, p. 162.

[14] Sandor Ferenczi, 1873–1933, a favorite pupil of Freud's who later went his own way in psychoanalysis.

[15] Freud, *Totem and Taboo*, p. 131. Ferenczi's report appeared in English as "A Little Chanticleer" in *Contributions to Psycho-Analysis*, 1916, p. 270.

[16] It has not been possible to determine whether or not this actually happened.

[17] "The Philosophy of Friedrich Nietzsche as a Psychopathological Problem," in *Friedrich Nietzsche: Fighter for Freedom*, GA 5, (Englewood, NJ: Rudolf Steiner Publications, 1960).

Lecture Five
SEXUALITY AND MODERN CLAIRVOYANCE:
FREUDIAN PSYCHOANALYSIS
AND SWEDENBORG AS A SEER

[1] Freud, *Totem and Taboo*. See Lecture Four, note 5.

[2] Ibid., p. 28.

[3] Ibid., p. 28.

[4] Rudolf Steiner, *Philosophy of Freedom: A Philosophy of Spiritual Activity*, GA 4, (London: Rudolf Steiner Press, 1988).

[5] In a lecture given in Dornach, August 8, 1915. See Lecture Three, note 8.

[6] It is a Masonic custom to give the neophyte two pairs of white gloves at the occasion of his admission. One is for himself, the other for the woman he reveres most highly.

Lecture Six

THE CONCEPT OF LOVE AS IT RELATES TO MYSTICISM

[1] Plutarch, c.46–after 119 A.D. Greek biographer and writer. In his work "On Isis and Osiris," Plutarch makes the distinction between the two on the basis of the origin of Venus and Amor. He uses the Greek "Eros" for "Amor."

[2] For instance, in a lecture given in Berlin on May 14, 1912, Lecture 6 in *Earthly and Cosmic Man*, GA 133, (London: Rudolf Steiner Publishing Company, 1948).

[3] Fritz Mauthner, 1849–1923, linguistic philosopher whose most important works were *Beiträge zu einer Kritik der Sprache*, 3 volumes, (Stuttgart and Berlin: 1901–1902) and *Wörterbuch der Philosophie. Neue Beiträge zu einer Kritik der Sprache*, 2 volumes, (Munich and Leipzig, 1910).

[4] *Knowledge of Higher Worlds*, see Lecture Three, note 6.

[5] *Theosophy*, see Lecture Two, note 10.

[6] The reference is to a line from Goethe's *Faust*: "Schau alle Wirkenskraft und Samen und tu nicht mehr in Worten kramen," "[I] may contemplate all seminal forces—and be done with peddling empty words." Johann Wolfgang von Goethe, *Faust*, trans. Stuart Atkins, (Cambridge, MA: Suhrkamp/Insel, 1984), Part One, Scene I, ll. 384–385.

[7] In all probability, the reference is to Laurenz Müllner (1848–1911), a Catholic theologian and professor of philosophy Rudolf Steiner met in Vienna in the salon of Marie Eugenie delle Grazie. See *The Course of My Life*, GA 28, (Hudson, NY: Anthroposophic Press, 1986) and *Vom Menschenrätsel* ("On the Riddle of the Human Being"), GA 20, (Dornach, Switzerland: Rudolf Steiner Verlag, 1984). [Not published in English—Translator].

[8] In German, "his pigtail hangs behind him." The reference is to a poem by Adalbert von Chamisso (1781–1838).

[9] The quotations on the following pages are from Mauthner's *Wörterbuch der Philosophie*, see note 3 above.

[10] Lou Andreas-Salomé, 1861–1937, German writer. Daughter of a German general in the service of the Russians, wife of Orientalist F. C. Andreas, a friend of Nietzsche and Rilke, with connections to Freud and psychoanalysis. She wrote novels, short stories, and nonfiction.

[11] Lou Andreas-Salomé, *Friedrich Nietzsche in seinen Werken*, ("Friedrich Nietzsche in His Writings"), 1894.

[12] See Address of August 21, 1915, in Part Two of this volume, p. 141.

[13] Arthur Schopenhauer, *The World as Will and Representation*, trans. E. F. J. Payne, (Indian Hills, Colorado: Falcon's Wing Press, 1958), Vol. II, Addenda to Book 4, Chapter 44, "Metaphysics of Sexual Love." This passage is also quoted in Mauthner's *Wörterbuch der Philosophie* in the entry on "Love."

[14] No stenographic record was kept of this meeting, since Rudolf Steiner did not participate in it.

Lecture Seven
THE PHILOSOPHY OF PSYCHOANALYSIS
AS ILLUMINATED BY AN ANTHROPOSOPHICAL
UNDERSTANDING OF THE HUMAN BEING

[1] Rudolf Steiner, *An Outline of Occult Science*, GA 13, repr., (Hudson, NY: Anthroposophic Press, 1989).

[2] See note 10 to Lecture 4 above.

PART TWO

I
THE PROTAGONISTS

[1] Alice Sprengel, b. 1871 in Scotland, d. 1949 in Bern, Switzerland. Grew up in Yorkshire, then came to Berlin and was active there in theosophical circles. There she also met Steiner and eventually joined his anthroposophical group and was a member of his Mystica Aeterna Lodge. After leaving Steiner, she joined the Order of Oriental Templars, a pseudo-masonic occult order. She became the secretary of Theodor Reuss (1855–1923), the Grand Master of the O.T.O. and moved with him and his group to Ascona. She was part of the Executive Council of the O.T.O., and by 1937 she was in charge of a Lodge of the O.T.O. in Locarno. For more information see Ellic Howe, *The Magicians of the Golden Dawn: A Documentary History of a Magical Order 1887–1923*, (London: Routledge & Kegan Paul, 1972) and Helmut

Möller and Ellic Howe, *Merlin Peregrinus: Vom Untergrund des Abendlandes* ("Merlin Peregrinus: On the Underground of the Occident"), (Würzburg: Königshausen & Neumann, 1986).

[2] From Rudolf Steiner's mystery drama *The Guardian of the Threshold* (Scene 4, Strader speaking to Theodora), *The Four Mystery Plays*, GA 14, (London: Rudolf Steiner Press, 1982), p. 297.

[3] The reference is to Edouard Schuré's drama *La Sœur Gardienne*. Rudolf Steiner began working on the production in the summer of 1913 in Munich, but had to abandon the project because he was overtaxed.

[4] Mary Peet Bivar, an Englishwoman living in Brussels, had been a pupil of Annie Besant's for many years before siding with Rudolf Steiner in 1910. She founded the Johannes Branch in Brussels in 1912, moved in the middle of 1914 first to Basel and then to Arlesheim. She was tirelessly active on behalf of Rudolf Steiner and anthroposophy until her death in 1927. See the obituary in *Was in der Anthroposophischen Gesellschaft vorgeht*, No. 44, October 30, 1927.

[5] See Karl Heyers, *Wie Man Gegen Rudolf Steiner Kämpft* ("How Rudolf Steiner Is Opposed"), Stuttgart, 1932.

[6] Paul Fechter, *Menschen und Zeiten: Begegnungen aus fünf Jahrzehnten* ("People and Times: Encounters in Five Decades"), Gütersloh, 1948.

[7] See Emanuel Hurwitz, *Otto Gross: Paradies-Sucher zwischen Freud und Jung* ("Otto Gross: Paradise-Seeker between Freud and Jung"), Zurich, 1979.

[8] In *Deutsche Rundschau*, May 1930.

[9] Max Asch, physician, died 1911. Member of the German Section of the Theosophical Society since 1904. While commemorating the dead during the General Assembly of 1911 (December 10, 1911), Rudolf Steiner dedicated these words to him:

"I must also recall a third person, whose departure from the physical plane may have seemed to many to have come unexpectedly quickly. This person is our beloved member Dr. Max Asch. In his extremely eventful life he had to overcome many things that can make it difficult for someone to approach a purely spiritual movement, but in the end he did find his way to us, and he, the physician, found healing for his own suffering in reading and studying theosophy. He assured me repeatedly that in his physician's heart he could find no more fruitful faith in any remedy than in what he received spiritually from theosophical books, that he could feel theosophical teachings streaming like balsam into his pain-racked body. He cultivated theosophy in this sense right up to the hour of his death. When our friend departed this world, it was very difficult for me to resign myself to not being able to speak a few words at the graveside as his daughter wrote to ask me. I was unable to fulfill this wish because my lecture series in Prague began that day, thus making it impossible for me to render this last service on the physical plane to our friend the theosophist. You can be sure that the words I would have spoken at his grave followed him in thought into the worlds he was entering."

Asch was also a friend of the physician Carl Ludwig Schleich (1859–1922). In this regard, see Rudolf Steiner's lecture given in Dornach on September 7, 1924, in *Karmic Relationships*, Vol. IV, GA 238, rev. ed. (London: Rudolf Steiner Press, 1983), pp.25–37.

10 In Vol. II of *Metamorphosis of the Soul: Paths of Experience*, GA 59, (London: Rudolf Steiner Press, 1983), pp. 85–100.

II
ADDRESS BY RUDOLF STEINER

1 Lecture of August 20, 1915, Dornach, entitled "Episodische Betrachtungen über Raum, Zeit, Bewegung" ("Some Observations on Space, Time, and Movement"), in *Der Wert des Denkens für eine den Menschen befriedigende Weltanschauung. Das Verhältnis der Geisteswissenschaft zur Naturwissenschaft* ("Thinking's Value for a Humanly Satisfying World View: The Relationship of Spiritual Science to Natural Science"), GA 164, (Dornach, Switzerland: Rudolf Steiner Verlag, 1984). [This lecture has not been published in English—Translator.]

2 Rudolf Steiner, "Gedanken während der Zeit des Krieges" ("Thoughts during the Time of War"), essay of July 5, 1915, in *Aufsätze über die Dreigliederung des sozialen Organismus und zur Zeitlage: Schriften und Aufsätze 1915–1921* ("On the Threefolding of the Social Organism and on the Current Situation: Essays and Articles 1915–1921"), GA 24, (Dornach, Switzerland: Rudolf Steiner Verlag, 1982). [Not available in English—Translator.]

3 Rudolf Steiner, *The Riddles of Philosophy*, GA 18, (Spring Valley, NY: Anthroposophic Press, 1973).

4 See p. 115 in this volume.

5 Address in Berlin, December 15, 1911, in *Zur Geschichte und aus den Inhalten der ersten Abteilung der Esoterischen Schule 1904 bis 1919* ("On the History and Contents of the First Class of the Esoteric School, 1904–1919"), GA 264, (Dornach, Switzerland: Rudolf Steiner Verlag, 1984). [This volume has not been published in English—Translator.]

6 Rudolf Steiner may well have been referring to his description of different types of clairvoyance, and especially the difference between "head clairvoyance" and "gut clairvoyance." Cf. the lecture series *Wege der Geistigen Erkenntniss und der Erneuerung künstlerischer Weltanschauung* ("Paths to Spiritual Knowledge and Renewal of Art Philosophy"), GA 161, (Dornach, Switzerland: Rudolf Steiner Verlag, 1980), and *Kunst- und Lebensfragen im Lichte der Geisteswissenschaft* ("Questions of Art and Life in the Light of Spiritual Science"), GA 162, (Dornach, Switzerland: Rudolf Steiner Verlag, 1985). [These volumes have not been published in English—Translator]

7 Hilde Boos-Hamburger in *Mitteilungen aus der anthroposophischen Arbeit in Deutschland* ("News about the Anthroposophical Work in Germany"), Vol 17, no. 1, Easter 1963.

8 Michael Bauer, 1871–1929, leader of the Albrecht Dürer Branch in Nürnberg. He was a member of the *Vorstand* of the Anthroposophical Society from 1913 until his retirement for health reasons in 1921.

III
ADDRESS BY RUDOLF STEINER

1 It has not been possible to ascertain which physician and which letter are referred to here.

2 See the volume *Zur Geschichte und aus den Inhalten der ersten Abteilung der Esoterischen Schule 1904 bis 1919*, note 5 to section II above.

3 See II, note 1 above.

4 See the two volumes *Geisteswissenschaftliche Erläuterungen zu Goethes "Faust"* ("Spiritual Scientific Commentaries on Goethe's *Faust*"), GA 272 and 273, (Dornach, Switzerland: Rudolf Steiner Verlag, 1981). [These volumes have not been published in English—Translator.]

5 Robert Hamerling, 1830–1889, Austrian poet.

[6] This seems to be a reference to Heinrich Goesch, who was not involved in any kind of practical activity. It was reported by some members that he had refused to help with the construction of the first Goetheanum.

[7] The person referred to is Alice Sprengel. See Part Two, p. 109ff in this volume and also note 1 under I above.

[8] The second half of this sentence is somewhat unclear in the stenographic record and may have not have been taken down exactly or completely.

[9] This letter has not been found.

IV

RESOLVING THE CASE

[1] Laura Marholm, pseudonym of Laura Hansson, née Mohr, 1854–1928, Swedish author whose books were published in German.

[2] Marie Madeleine, pseudonym of M. M. von Puttkamer, 1881–? Caused a sensation with books published around the turn of the century because of her advocacy of free love.

[3] Dolorosa, pseudonym of Maria Eichhorn, 1879–? poet and novelist.

[4] Margarete Beutler, M. Friedrich-Freska, née Beutler, 1884–1949. Under the pseudonym Margit Friedrich, she wrote lyric poetry and stories on social themes.

[5] Julia Wernicke, Member of the Anthroposophical Society, no further details known.

[6] Mieta (Pyle-)Waller, 1883–1954. Since about 1907, a friend and close artiotic colleague of Marie Steiner-von Sivers and Rudolf Steiner.

[7] Mrs. von Strauss, Member of the Anthroposophical Society, no further details known.

Publisher's Note

THE LECTURES and addresses printed here were given by
Rudolf Steiner to audiences familiar with the general background and terminology of his anthroposophical teaching. It
should be remembered that in his autobiography *The Course of
My Life*, he emphasizes the distinction between his written
works on the one hand, and on the other, reports of lectures
that were given as oral communications and were not originally
intended for print. For an intelligent appreciation of the lectures
it should be borne in mind that certain premises were taken for
granted when the words were spoken. "These premises,"
Rudolf Steiner writes, "include at the very least the anthroposophical knowledge of Man and of the Cosmos in its spiritual
essence; also what may be called 'anthroposophical history,'
told as an outcome of research into the spiritual world."